**insight text guide**

Melanie Van Langenberg

# Things a Map Won't Show You

Edited by
Susan La Marca
& Pam Macintyre

First published in 2023, reprinted in 2024, 2025.

Insight Publications Pty Ltd
3/350 Charman Road
Cheltenham VIC 3192
Australia
Tel: +61 3 8571 4950
Email: books@insightpublications.com.au

**www.insightpublications.com.au**

A catalogue record for this book is available from the National Library of Australia

*Susan La Marca & Pam Macintyre (eds), Things a Map Won't Show You /*
Melanie Van Langenberg

Melanie Van Langenberg asserts the moral right to be identified as the author of this work.

ISBNs:
9781922771933 (print)
9781922771940 (digital)

Cover design by Hayley Sinnatt

Printed by Markono Print Media Pte Ltd

# contents

# STORY MAP

**'Out of the Yellow'**
family, siblings, wonder, nature, holidays

**'The Two Little Round Stones'**
nature, First Nations cultures, storytelling

**'The Price of a Sword'**
power, honour, transformation, culture, parental expectations, family, siblings

**'The Exotic Rissole'**
culture, transformation, friendship, family, self-acceptance

**'Learning to Fly'**
dreams, parents, discovery

**'Australia Day'**
family, celebrations, coming of age, self-discovery

**'Only a Game'**
acceptance, community, culture, discovery

**'Snow Falls on the Subway'**
nature, community, wonder

**'Smarty'**
growing up, discovery, self-acceptance, family

**'The Second-Last Baby Tooth'**
family, holidays, growing up, coming of age

**'The Legend of Lungalunga'**
community, fear, storytelling

**'Chewing Gum'**
growing up, culture, family, identity, shame

**'A Dozen Bloomin' Roses'**
bullying, friendship, acceptance, gender, discovery, romance, shame

**'How I Taught My Grandmother to Read'**
culture, education, knowledge, family, acceptance, identity

**'Cloud Busting'**
nature, family, siblings, friendship, First Nations cultures, race

**'Milford Sound'**
nature, parental expectations, race, identity, trauma, coming of age, transformation

**'Ice-Cream Headache'**
culture, communication, transformation, self-discovery

**'The True Story of Mary'**
acceptance, friendship, family

**'Integration'**
acceptance, humanity

**Poems of Horiguchi Daigaku**
nature, emotions, discovery

**'Stark's Statues'**
culture, discovery, art

**'Introducing Wendy'**
friendship, romance, discovery, self-confidence

**'Smiley'**
acceptance, family, transformation

**'The Year King'**
customs, power, problem-solving, education, knowledge, government, community

**'Yinti's Kitten'**
nature, First Nations cultures, siblings, family

**'The Art of Hunting'**
nature, First Nations cultures, customs, respect

**'A Guide to Better Kissing for Australian Teens'**
culture, customs, relationships

**'All One Race'**
humanity, acceptance

# OVERVIEW

## About the editors

**Dr Susan La Marca** is currently the Executive Officer of the School Library Association of Victoria (SLAV). One of her responsibilities in this role involves the production of the *Synergy* research journal, which explores the importance of school librarianship, where she serves as editor. She also provides consulting work in the areas of young adult literature and library services. La Marca is the co-editor of *Where the Shoreline Used to Be: Stories from Australia and Beyond* (2016) and co-author of *Knowing Readers: Unlocking the Pleasures of Reading* (2006), both with Dr Pam Macintyre. She is also the author of *Designing the Learning Environment: Learning in a Changing World* (2010) and editor of *Rethink!: Ideas for Inspiring School Library Design* (2007).

La Marca has previously worked as Head of Library and Information Services at Genazzano FCJ College in Melbourne, and as the Regional Director of Oceania for the International Association of School Librarianship (IASL). Her PhD work at the University of Melbourne focused on how to create a reading environment and the role of the teacher-librarian as an enabling adult. She is a strong advocate for teacher-librarians and the role they play in enriching the reading experiences of young people, as well as for promoting the value of school libraries and their staff.

**Dr Pam Macintyre** is a Senior Lecturer at RMIT University, teaching language and literacy, and children's and young adult literature. She is the founding editor of *Viewpoint: On Books for Young Adults*, a publication of The University of Melbourne, and writes for *Australian Book Review*. With Stella Lees, Macintyre co-edited *The Oxford Companion to Australian Children's Literature* (1993), an encyclopedic reference with 1600 entries. She is also co-editor of *Where the Shoreline*

*Used to Be: Stories from Australia and Beyond* (2016) and co-author of *Knowing Readers: Unlocking the Pleasures of Reading* (2006), both with Susan La Marca.

Macintyre has been the recipient of the Dromkeen Librarian's Award for Services to Children's Literature and the Leila St John Award for Distinguished Services to Children's Literature. She has also served as a judge for the Victorian Premier's Literary Awards, the Children's Book Council of Australia Book of the Year Awards, and the Aurealis Awards (Australia's premier speculative fiction awards).

## Synopsis

*Things a Map Won't Show You: Stories from Australia and Beyond* is a collection of twenty-eight independent pieces including short stories, illustrations, poetry, a brochure and a graphic short story. The overarching premise of the collection is to reveal the heart and soul of communities and their people, beyond the physical landscape revealed by a map.

Nearly all the central figures of the narratives are young people trying to learn who they are amid various trials or family circumstances. Most of the stories focus upon a turning point in a young person's life, where they cross a threshold in their coming of age, or into a realisation that changes them. Parents and guardians feature in many stories, portrayed varyingly as kind and supportive or unsympathetic and spurning (rejecting), although the latter is mostly true of the more comical poems in the collection. These stories are united by their consideration of relationships, whether that be to family, friends, a place, the land or oneself.

# BACKGROUND & CONTEXT

The twenty-eight stories that appear in *Things a Map Won't Show You: Stories from Australia and Beyond* are created by a range of writers, from emerging to established. Some of the stories were published for the first time in this collection, while others appeared in previous collections or are extracts from longer texts.

As the title suggests, most of the stories are set in Australia. Some stories are set in other countries, including New Zealand, China, Japan, India, Papua New Guinea and Korea. The stories celebrate a variety of cultures, with protagonists coming from a range of backgrounds while calling Australia home. Six of the stories are by First Nations writers. Drawing from a variety of voices was a specific intention of La Marca and Macintyre's in curating this collection. As they explain in their introduction, they hoped the stories would broaden readers' understandings of culture and identity, and 'offer a different way of seeing the world'. Above all, the stories inspire an appreciation of the difficulties, but ultimate triumphs, involved in developing a sense of belonging.

Most of the stories are set within an indeterminate (unknown) time period with only a few being clearly placed within a specific year or era.

- The shift in narrative perspective takes Tara June Winch's 'Cloud Busting' to 1967.
- Mentions of the end of the gold rush place Peta Freestone's 'Milford Sound' in the late nineteenth century.
- The epigraphs that precede Alison Lloyd's 'The Price of a Sword' indicate that the story is set near 210 BCE.
- The reference to people enjoying Triveni's writing forty years after her passing sets Sudha Murty's 'How I Taught My Grandmother to Read' in 2003.

# GENRE, STRUCTURE & LANGUAGE

## Genre

*Things a Map Won't Show You* includes a diverse range of genres across the stories in the collection. While the majority may be seen as realistic fiction, others could be categorised as historical fiction, humour, romance, adventure, myths and legends, suspense, bildungsroman (a coming-of-age story) or fantasy. Indeed, many of the stories work across genre.

Genre is also sometimes considered as the form taken by a particular text. In this sense, the pieces in this collection include short stories, poetry and transcribed oral storytelling, as well as a graphic short story and a brochure.

Acknowledging the genre of a given story can help with understanding the conventions within which they have been created and align. For example, a story like Paul Jennings' 'A Dozen Bloomin' Roses' is reflective of the suspense genre, among others. It therefore includes elements such as conflict, red herrings and an ominous tone. Another example is that of 'The Second-Last Baby Tooth' by Sonya Hartnett. As a story that could be categorised as a bildungsroman, it includes elements such as an inciting incident, a transformation in maturity or understanding by the central character, and a supportive older figure who acts as a guide.

## Structure

There are two main ways of considering structure when studying a collection of stories. There is the structure of the overall collection, in terms of how La Marca and Macintyre have chosen to order the stories, and then there is the structure of the individual texts.

*Things a Map Won't Show You* opens with James Roy's 'Out of the Yellow'. A dominant idea here is the narrator Alex's preoccupation with the map that charts the family's journey from their wheat farm to the coast. What 'really blows [his] mind is the distance around the country, the distance along the wiggly black line which divides the yellow land from the pale blue sea' (p.8). Later, upon arriving at the coast, standing in the 'damp sand' (p.13), Alex is taken by the notion that 'this is what the black wiggly line means – this very spot is somewhere on it' (p.13). This could serve as a metaphor for standing on the cusp of understanding, of wonder, of experience; the same position the reader is in before they embark on the rest of the collection.

The collection itself celebrates both diversity and unity. After reading stories that validate, affirm, broaden and challenge the readers' own experiences, La Marca and Macintyre close their collection with 'All One Race' by Oodgeroo Noonuccal. Having read such a wide-ranging selection of stories, readers are roused to recognise the shared humanity that exists regardless of perceived, superficial differences.

Analysing the structure of individual stories includes considering elements such as the narrative structure as well as construction elements such as illustrations, narrative viewpoints and use of setting.

### Narrative structure

Most of the stories in the collection follow a linear time line, where readers experience the story in the same order as the events actually unfold. Some stories have a nonlinear structure, which is when the plot events are presented out of order so that the story moves back and forward in time, such as in 'Only a Game' by Ruth Starke. While not nonlinear, the narrative in Paul Jennings' 'A Dozen Bloomin' Roses' foreshadows later events, creating a sense of suspense as the reader is eager to uncover how events are connected.

### Illustrations and the graphic short story

'Stark's Statues' (Tohby Riddle), 'The Legend of Lungalunga' (Samson Tavat), 'Yinti's Kitten' (Pat Lowe and Jimmy Pike) and 'The Art of Hunting' (Brenton McKenna) include illustrations as part of their story. 'Stark's Statues' and 'The Art of Hunting' would be considered multimodal stories, as the written and visual language work together in order to convey the narrative; the stories would be unclear or nonsensical if one element was missing.

When analysing stories that include illustrations, particularly multimodal stories, it is important to consider how the illustrations add to the meaning-making of the story and how they enhance the writer's ability to convey their message.

### Narrative viewpoints

The narrative voice can be presented in several ways. If the narrative is told through the voice of a character within the story, this is a character-bound or first-person narration. A narrative that is related by an omniscient voice removed from the action of the story is an external narrator, which may centre on observing a particular character or move between the perspectives of a variety of characters. This can also be called third-person narration. Another form of narrative voice is second-person narration, which is when the narrator uses the word 'you' to speak directly to the reader.

Stories within *Things a Map Won't Show You* vary in the narrative voices in which they are told. The majority of the stories, such as 'Learning to Fly' (Sofie Laguna), 'The Second-Last Baby Tooth' (Sonya Hartnett) and 'Chewing Gum' (anonymous), encourage the reader to empathise more closely with the experiences of the characters through their use of character-bound narration. There are also many stories that are related through external (omniscient) narration, where readers experience the stories from a distance.

Four stories in the collection use second-person narration: 'Out of the Yellow' (James Roy), 'Ice-Cream Headache' (Tim Sinclair),

'Integration' (Jack Davis) and 'A Guide to Better Kissing for Australian Teens' (Chris Wheat). The 'you' unavoidably merges with the identity of the reader, thus making it feel as though they are experiencing these events themselves. This can make the resonance (impact) and power of the story stronger, though can also be somewhat alienating for some.

### Setting

While, on a broad scale, these stories are set in 'Australia and beyond', the physical, geographic, social and cultural contexts are also important factors in appreciating various nuances. Characters are conditioned by the contexts in which they exist, often being a product of their time. Kerr and Abigail McNevin, of 'Milford Sound' (Peta Freestone), live in the late nineteenth century, thus attitudes towards gender roles, race and the environment, among other things, are not the same as attitudes of the twenty-first century. Cultural and spiritual customs within Aboriginal groups help to inform nomadic lifestyles, hunting and values, as is explored in stories such as 'Yinti's Kitten' (Pat Lowe and Jimmy Pike) and 'The Art of Hunting' (Brenton McKenna). The high respect afforded parents, teachers and elders in some cultures informs the magnitude of shame and embarrassment felt by a child who is caught stealing, like in 'Chewing Gum' (anonymous).

The physical space in which a story is set can also be symbolic of broader ideas that the writer is encouraging their reader to consider. For example, in setting the climactic moments of 'A Dozen Bloomin' Roses' on an enclosed train, Jennings heightens the suffocating shame that Gerald is feeling and draws attention to the extent to which he feels his current situation is inescapable.

## Language

Writers make many careful decisions in crafting their stories, using language as evocatively as possible to help guide readers to think and feel in different ways. Some of these decisions involve the use of analogies, metaphors, similes, symbolism, personification, rhyming and more.

Many of the stories in this collection revolve around the idea of growing up, and the writers have found different ways to help readers associate the ideas within their story with the broader concept of coming of age. For example, in 'The Second-Last Baby Tooth', the protagonist loses their second-last baby tooth moments after they acknowledge how defeated they feel by childhood. They believe that 'a kid's world is small and simple' (p.198) and they want to live in the other world where 'everything was sensible, where there were answers to all the mysteries' (p.198). Hartnett uses the lost baby tooth to symbolise that this young person is on the precipice of growing up but nature is making them hold on a little bit longer. James Roy uses the map in 'Out of the Yellow' to symbolise a similar idea.

Peta Freestone presents the titular Milford Sound of her story as a formidable force, with those who think themselves above the might of the Sound and the gods incurring its wrath. In personifying the Sound, Freestone makes it seem like a separate character with feelings, responses and motivations of its own.

Using comparisons and contrasts can also guide readers to make associations between various ideas, characters or experiences. In 'Only a Game', Ruth Starke establishes the setting of the 'Alternative Place of Detention' (p.127) by drawing attention to the number of ways in which it is similar to the place where the children from North Illaba Primary School live. In mentioning that the houses 'looked remarkably like the houses [Lan] and his friends lived in' (p.121) or that there was a tricycle just like the one Lan's sister plays with, perceived gaps or differences between these two groups may be bridged.

By identifying the language choices and the way that writers use language to craft ideas, you will deepen your understanding of the meaning within these stories.

# STORY-BY-STORY ANALYSIS

## 'Out of the Yellow' by James Roy (pp.3–13)

**Summary:** *Alex and his sister Kellie are on their first family trip to the coast, from their home on a wheat farm in New South Wales. Kellie is eagerly anticipating seeing the ocean for the first time while Alex is tempering his enthusiasm, nearing on apathy. His sense of wonder shifts markedly when they finally make it to the beach in Sydney.*

Roy's story uses the juxtaposing attitudes of the siblings Alex and Kellie toward their imminent first visit to the coast, to highlight the awe and admiration that the natural world can inspire. Kellie is 'so excited about going to the beach' (p.7), incessantly talking about it for the entire trip, even to the point of creating conversations with herself when her family tires of her repetitiveness. However, when the family finally gets to the beach, Kellie appears quite composed and relaxed, perhaps alluding to the calming power of nature. Initially thinking that 'it's not really such a big deal' (p.3), upon arrival at the beach Alex is absolutely transfixed: his 'gaze fixed on the ocean' (p.12). Through this, Roy portrays Alex as emerging from this family holiday changed.

Alex's development is also evident through his interest in the map used on their travels. In travelling to the 'very edge of the country' (p.13), Alex is also awakened from the insular world he once cultivated for himself, now interested in what exists beyond.

***Q*** 'This is where Australia ends and the rest of the world begins.' Why do you think Alex is so preoccupied with thinking about the 'edge of the map' (p.13)?

***Q*** Write about a time where the reality of an experience exceeded your expectations.

## 'Cloud Busting' by Tara June Winch (pp.17–23)

**Summary:** *The unnamed narrator's mother recalls how her own mother, Alice, saved up enough money, over a period of 'three years and seven months' (p.21), to buy a set of 'five different size pans and a Dutch oven' (p.20). This purchase was achieved through the help of a travelling salesman named Samuel who collected the payment every month, and who became her mother's friend. Samuel delivers the set with a full meal cooked within each item: a kind gesture that moves both Alice and the narrator's mother.*

'Cloud busting' serves as a metaphor for the way that love and human connection can create light and joy during difficult times. The story commences with the narrator and their sibling going cloud busting, an activity that involves joining hands so that they can 'build up the biggest brightest rainbow' (p.17) and shoot it up into the sky to 'bust' clouds. This sets up the definition of the story's title while also positioning readers to engage with the story's main narrative in a particular way: the friendship that develops between Alice and Samuel bursts through the struggles of dealing with life's challenges. For Alice, living in 1967 Australia involved economic hardship but, mostly, the struggles of being separated from all but one of her children, presumably as part of the stolen generations.

Winch also emphasises the importance of storytelling as a means of helping culture, values and legacies survive. The saucepans and Dutch oven that feature in the main narrative have now been passed down two generations, as well as the stories that are known 'off by heart, over and over, every detail' (p.18).

### Key point

In May 1967 a referendum was held in which Australians voted to change the wording of the Constitution so that Aboriginal and Torres Strait Islander peoples were counted as part of the population of Australia. This provides some context to the significance of the friendship between Alice and Samuel.

### Key vocabulary

*Cockles:* an edible shelled mollusc.

*Missions:* housing for Aboriginal and Torres Strait Islander peoples that was created by churches and religious individuals and used to indoctrinate them into accepting Christian beliefs and Western ideals and customs.

*Periwinkles:* an edible type of sea snail.

*Pipis:* an edible mollusc native to eastern Australia and New Zealand.

***Q*** '… maybe when those clouds burst open, he got to feel the rain. A cleansing rain, and maybe that was enough' (p.23). Whether as part of the siblings' game or figuratively for the friendship between Alice and Samuel, how is cloud busting cleansing for the characters in this story?

***Q*** Think of an heirloom that exists within your family. This could be a story or a physical item. What significance does this hold in your family's story?

## 'The Two Little Round Stones' by Obed Raggett (pp.27–8)

**Summary:** *Two boys go hunting and become frightened when they realise that they will be caught in heavy rain. They find shelter in two caves that form after they throw two stones that grow bigger and bigger, creating the boys' shelter for two nights. The boys discard these two stones when they find new replacements, but these do not have the same power and so, when the next heavy rain comes, the boys have no protection and they are killed.*

Raggett's tale acts as an allegory for the importance of not taking nature and its protection for granted. In doing so, humans are limiting their own prosperity. This is portrayed through the two boys discarding the two little round stones that had been a means of protection during heavy rains in favour of 'two better-looking ones' (p.28). This moral aligns with humanity's current treatment of our natural world more generally, whereby natural resources are abused and discarded in favour of alternatives that appear more attractive but are, in fact, shortening our future.

***Q*** Write about two real-world examples with which the moral of this story aligns.

***Q*** Write an allegory connected to a real-world issue of your choice.

## 'Milford Sound' by Peta Freestone (pp.31–47)

**Summary:** *Abigail McNevin lives with her widowed father, Kerr, who steals and sells greenstone from the Sound. Abigail's friend and romantic interest, Ikaw, believes that Kerr's actions have aroused 'the anger of the gods down on his family' (p.39), evident through the death of Abigail's mother. When Abigail's father also dies and she discovers his hoard of greenstone, she tries to dispose of it but, on her final trip, she falls into the Sound. The story finishes with Abigail returning home, sick and injured, where she recuperates and eventually feels hopeful about her future.*

This is one of the few stories not set in Australia, with Freestone's story taking place in New Zealand in the late nineteenth century. Abigail is a fourteen-year-old with a bourgeoning (growing) sense of independence, inspired by the example set by her late mother. It is shown that her mother was a strong and formidable woman who 'didn't care that [cutting peat] was men's work' (p.37), thus defying gender norms of the time. Readers see this strength begin to emerge in Abigail through the way that she speaks up to her father about topics such as weather conditions and the power of the Sound, regardless of the fear and timidness that he inspires in her. Abigail also disobeys her father's strict orders of keeping 'better company than that half-caste Maori boy' (p.33), by pursuing a relationship with him, even harbouring the idea of one day becoming Ikaw's wife.

## Key point

The term 'half-caste' is now regarded as offensive; historically, it was used in Australia as a race-based term that classified First Nations peoples of mixed ethnicity. It was widely used in New Zealand during the period 'Milford Sound' is set in, and Freestone uses this word in Kerr's dialogue to convey his racist and discriminatory behaviours.

Grief plays a significant role in the dynamic between father and daughter, as well as acting as a burden in their lives. Abigail acknowledges that her father blames her for her mother's death; 'he never says it, but [she knows] he does' (p.38). Freestone also scatters references to copper curls throughout the story, creating connections between the mother and daughter's appearances, and thus a reminder of the father and daughter's loss. The death of her father, however, elicits no immediate reaction from Abigail, leaving her to '[wonder] if that meant she was evil' (p.44). At the story's close, as Abigail hallucinates visions of her mother and father, Freestone implies that she is finally able to accept and be at peace with her grief, with the 'cool, calm water of the Sound' (p.47).

A dominant idea explored throughout Freestone's story is the way that those who abuse and destroy the natural world are punished, and the belief in a higher power. In spite of warnings that 'the gods are sad that the forests are being cut for the sheep and sawmills ... and mighty angry about [Kerr] disturbing the greenstone' (p.40) and that 'every late winter the Sound has taken someone' (p.40), Abigail's father greedily steals and sells greenstone. Ultimately, he is killed in the Sound. As a point of difference, Freestone shows that those who respect and fear the might of the Sound, like Ikaw, are kept safe.

### Key vocabulary

*Heretic:* a person whose religious beliefs or practices are contrary to those that are generally accepted.

*Peat:* a natural material used as fuel, created through the partial decomposition of vegetable matter in marshy environments such as bogs.

*Pounamu:* a valuable green gemstone found in New Zealand that Māori people use for crafting tools and ornaments.

*Sallying:* a defending military attack.

*Sound:* a deep, narrow body of water between land masses or larger bodies of water, which is usually connected to the sea.

*Tangiwai*: found in Milford Sound, this is a type of pounamu whose name refers to the Māori legend of a spirit guardian woman stolen from her husband who cries sorrowful, crystallised tears.

***Q*** Consider the ending of this story. Is it hopeful or is it ominous?

***Q*** Personify a natural setting within Australia or somewhere else in the world. How would it think or act towards the people that exist within it?

## 'The Price of a Sword' by Alison Lloyd (pp.51–62)

**Summary:** *Following his family's fall from power, Meng of the royal family of Yen attempts to improve the family's status by exchanging wine for a second-hand knife. He then decides to instead support his brother, Ger, in obtaining a 'slim Qin [sword], of tempered bronze' (p.56), that may serve as a gateway to the military academy. Initially reluctant, their father agrees to help Ger's ambition by giving a gift to the Wang family who run the Academy. The brothers don't realise, until it's too late, that the gift is their thirteen-year-old cousin Crimson-Silk's hand in marriage to the infant grand-nephew of General Wang.*

Another story set outside Australia, Lloyd's 'The Price of a Sword' centres on a family's drastic change in circumstance following the overthrow of the Yen family dynasty by the King of Qin in China. Pride, power and honour underpin many of the events of this story, primarily directed by Meng and Ger's father, who strives vehemently to uphold and reclaim the honour that was stolen from his family. Lloyd conveys the way pride can change an individual for the worse, making them inconsiderate of or blind to the emotions and needs of loved ones. The brothers' reluctance to confront their father about their goals is testament to this.

The way that a child's faith in a parental figure changes with age and experience is also explored. Meng and Ger become less trusting of their father's convictions, wondering how long it will take for them to return to Yen and the promised 'honour and glory' (p.51). They grow sceptical, too, of his judgements, something that is compounded for Meng when his beloved cousin is sold 'into Qin hands' (p.62) as 'the price of [their] dreams' (p.62).

The greatest emphasis in the story is on the idea that one's dreams can come at a price, as indicated through the story's title and its closing line. Lloyd warns readers that there are sacrifices involved in attaining particular goals and aspirations, but does not discourage readers from holding dreams. The cost of Meng and Ger's dreams here is attributed to naivety rather than an inherent hopelessness regarding ambition.

#### Key vocabulary

*Anvil:* a heavy iron block that has a flat top and concave sides.

***Q*** '... most of what gets bought and sold is invisible. It can't be weighed. But people will pay for it just the same. Like power, and respect' (pp.57–8). Discuss how the idea of power is explored throughout Lloyd's story.

***Q*** Imagine that Meng is able to write a letter to his cousin Crimson-Silk after her marriage into the Qin family. What would he write?

## 'Ice-Cream Headache' by Tim Sinclair (pp.65–73)

**Summary:** *An unnamed narrator stands in a Circle-K convenience store after arriving in Japan seven hours prior. The language barrier means that they struggle communicating their need for an aspirin to a store clerk and are sold an ice-cream instead. Though this is not what they wanted, the traveller is moved and comforted by the clerk's kindness.*

Sinclair's poem is set in Japan, seven hours after the narrator 'got off the plane' (p.66) there. It conveys the issues with communication and translation that the narrator experiences, but emphasises the way that kindness and humanity can transcend these obstacles.

Sinclair highlights the narrator's deep desire to escape and how they are 'flying away from a life / that [they] wanted to change' (p.67). These efforts are portrayed as overwhelming, with Sinclair drawing attention to the sensory overload that makes the protagonist feel overcome with how everything is so 'different' (p.68). A juxtaposition is presented between expectations and reality: 'nothing … working out / like [they] planned' (p.66). Like many of the stories, the poem's resolution celebrates the protagonist's transition and learning, and the impact that this has on their sense of self.

***Q*** Compare the experiences of the protagonist in 'Ice-Cream Headache' and Alex in 'Out of the Yellow'. How do their expectations and reality misalign? Compare what they learn.

***Q*** Think of a time where you were misunderstood. This might have been because of a language barrier or confused communication. How did this make you feel?

## 'The Exotic Rissole' by Tanveer Ahmed (pp.77–83)

**Summary:** *Daryl (Lynchy) is a constant visitor to his best friend Tanny's home, loving the Bangladeshi culture that abounds there, but Tanny has never visited Lynchy's home. Tanny is finally invited to Lynchy's home on the last day of primary school, after which the two boys will study at different schools. Tanny eagerly accepts this invitation, excited to 'fulfill [his] wish of tasting the mouth-watering promise of [Lynchy's] family's rissole' (p.80), something his own mother never cooks.*

Ahmed's story is a celebration of a cross-cultural friendship between Tanny, a child of Bangladeshi migrants, and Lynchy, a white Australian. A series of contrasts is presented between their respective family lives and cultures, but the strength of the trust and love between them is strong. Through this, Ahmed pays testament to the importance of having meaningful relationships that affirm one's identity, especially during the formative years.

There is also a strong sense of wonder that exists towards the markers of the other's culture, with Lynchy seeming 'to love hanging out at [Tanny's] house' (p.78) and Tanny excited when he is finally invited to Lynchy's home. Many points of difference are listed, ranging from parental behaviours, homes, smells and conversation, in addition to broader-scale differences based on race and class.

The innocence of childhood is also conveyed through the pre-technology games and activities that the two friends enjoy. Lynchy and Tanny would play every day after school, starting at Tanny's home and then riding their 'BMX bikes to the local creek ... [to] play marbles, skim rocks ... or play French cricket with a plastic bat' (p.78).

***Q*** 'It was a rare tender moment between two boys entering manhood' (p.81). Why is it important to have trusting relationships during one's formative years?

***Q*** Think about a significant friend with whom you have lost contact. Write them a letter detailing the importance of their friendship at that time in your lives.

## 'The True Story of Mary, who wanted to stand on her head' by Jane Godwin (pp.87–93)

**Summary:** *A young girl named Mary has the unusual compulsion to stand on her head. Perturbed by this, her parents seek medical intervention; however, this, and other 'Drastic Measures' (p.89) such as being exiled to the desert, result in no change. After she is expelled, Mary returns to the desert where she ultimately finds acceptance and happiness with a camel, a mouse and a lizard.*

A serious message about acceptance is hidden within the humour and frivolity of this poem's rhyming structure. Similar to two other poems in the collection, Doug MacLeod's 'Smarty' and 'Smiley', Godwin gives passing reference to parents who reject their child, albeit somewhat reluctantly, because she does not subscribe to the norms governing acceptable behaviour. In this case, Mary is deemed to have a 'behavioural disorder' (p.90) because she engages in 'an act of incongruousness' (p.87): standing on her head. Ultimately, Mary finds unreserved acceptance and friendship from a mouse, a camel and a lizard who occupy the same desert in which she had been abandoned by her parents.

The three animals are described as 'her soul mates – of which there were three' (p.92), language that is reminiscent of the way Mary's parents were introduced: 'parents (of which there were no more than two)' (p.87). This alludes to the familial alliance that one can find among good friends. Godwin makes it clear that this is a sad series of events that means Mary never sees her parents again; however, the story does celebrate the general importance of finding a place where 'there was nobody there not to let [Mary]' be herself (p.90). Thus, the need to have a sense of belonging, where one is accepted and celebrated regardless of perceived idiosyncrasies, and can be one's true self, is important.

***Q*** Compare and contrast the way Godwin presents Mary's parents and her animal friends. How does this impact the way readers perceive or respond to them?

***Q*** Think of a place or a group of people with whom you feel entirely comfortable to be yourself. Write a haiku that celebrates this.

## 'Learning to Fly' by Sofie Laguna (pp.97–100)

**Summary:** *David harbours (holds onto) the desperate dream to fly. In an attempt to do so, he falls off the roof of the shed, breaking his leg. In hospital, he receives a set of 'pencils, paints and a sketchbook' (p.99) from his class teacher. In discovering a love of painting, David feels that he has finally learned how to fly.*

The desire to fly, although literal for a time, serves as a metaphor for David's yearning for freedom, exploration and self-expression. Within the scope that dreams allow, he flies 'around the sun, beyond the moon into the starry universe' (p.97) and rejoices at the chance to 'go wherever [he] wanted' (p.97). In reality, there is nothing that affords him these same feelings of liberation. That is, until he discovers his inclination for painting, ironically, when he is grounded after jumping off the roof of his shed in an attempt to fly. Laguna presents David's moment of discovery with a sense of urgent recognition, with listing and repetition used to convey the sense of freedom that he finds through this new hobby.

***Q*** 'I felt heavy as a bird born without wings' (p.99). How does this simile convey the importance of flying, and eventually painting, for David?

***Q*** Write a short reflection about something in your life that makes you feel uninhibited and free to express your true self.

## 'Integration' by Jack Davis (pp.103–4)

**Summary:** *The narrator expresses their hope for a nation that celebrates the combination of two worlds and cultures.*

Davis acknowledges the pain and suffering that exists within and between the 'two worlds' (p.103) in Australia, referencing the violent colonial history in Australia that began when European colonisers arrived on the land where First Nations peoples had been living for tens of thousands of years. He offers a hopeful future, however, insisting that 'the past is done' (p.104) and that it is possible to 'forget the hurt' (p.103). Like Noonuccal's poem 'All One Race', which closes the collection, 'Integration' celebrates the unity and peace that could exist if we 'let these two worlds combine, yours and mine' (p.103).

### Key vocabulary

*Integration:* the combination of two things that were previously segregated.

***Q*** Davis says that 'there is no need … to build a wall to crouch and hide, / To cry or sneer behind' (p.103). What does he mean by this?

***Q*** Create a visual representation of the message behind this poem.

## 'Australia Day' by Ursula Dubosarsky (pp.107–13)

**Summary:** *An unnamed narrator relates the events of Australia Day in the year they turned ten. Their parents invite their strange neighbour Mrs Banks to lunch, who steers the conversation to her fascination with ants and her belief that Shakespeare wrote the Bible. After eating too many potatoes at lunch, the narrator is visited by a doctor who convinces them that they have been poisoned and are dying, and they are unable to join in with the public holiday celebrations.*

Dubosarsky's story explores the nature of childhood uncertainty. After fainting during lunch and the doctor pronouncing that the child has 'been poisoned' (p.110), the unnamed narrator is left at home while their family 'strolled down to the local oval' (p.111) to enjoy Australia Day celebrations. Left alone, their mind travels a circuitous route pondering the meaning of life. The day has involved many things that the protagonist has felt beyond their comprehension. From confusing tales shared by their neighbour and the quietness of their parents, to their imagined-deathbed musings, the protagonist eventually feels at a loss as to what their purpose in life will be.

However, Dubosarsky ends the story on a comforting note, reflecting the sense of wonder and peace that can come when one accepts their own naivety and ignorance. The narrator decides that they want to keep on living, not letting the poisoning be their end, and sees their future years 'suddenly laid out in the night sky … stretching off into the extraordinary distance, constantly moving forward, like a long line of diligent, determined ants' (p.113). Through this, Dubosarsky presents childhood as a time for wonder, experimentation and hope, using the night sky as analogous to the scope and direction of a life's purpose.

This story makes some significant references to the history behind the date of Australia Day. This national holiday marks the arrival of British colonisers in Australia when Governor Phillip landed with the First Fleet in Sydney Cove in 1788. Dubosarsky describes 'Governor Phillip in his red coat … scanning the new world' as well as 'the famous botanist Sir

Joseph Banks' (p.112), both key colonial figures. She also alludes to the immense harm and cruelty that ensued through colonisation, with the protagonist not being able to enjoy the Australia Day celebrations and comparing the sounds to 'battlefields and soldiers' and 'funerals in their hundreds, and their thousands and even hundreds of thousands' (p.112). The protagonist also reflects on how there were 'too many boats in the world', and poses the question: 'Why didn't people just stay at home?' (p.112).

***Q*** What is the significance of Mrs Banks' inclusion in this story?

***Q*** Write a short story about how your family celebrates a particular holiday.

## Poems by Horiguchi Daigaku (pp.117–18)

**Summary:** *'Sea Scene' evokes images of the sights and sounds of the sea, such as through comparing it to a meadow. 'Poetry' muses on the power that poems have to create meaning. 'I Know That Intense Emotion' conjures images of nature, equated to intense desires and emotions.*

The three poems by Daigaku share a common idea of celebrating the minutiae that combine to make a whole. A sea scene is conveyed through the evocation of a seagull, waves and a steamer, with Daigaku appealing to the reader's senses through using metaphors, similes and personification with each component. A poem is made analogous to a house, highlighting the integral role each word plays in building meaning: 'Each line supporting the other, each word / Echoing through its neighbour' (p.118). The intricacies of intense emotion are portrayed as heightened variations of love, wonder and sympathy.

### Key vocabulary

*Pothooks:* hooks that are shaped like the letter 'S'.

*Steamer:* a type of ship that is powered by steam.

***Q*** Consider the way Daigaku uses analogy and metaphor throughout these three poems. How do these help to create an image or visual of the overall ideas and enhance meaning?

***Q*** Find a photograph of a setting. You might consider a scene like the beach, a busy city street, a park or a playground. Choose three individual parts of this scene that are integral to creating this setting. Write a poem that celebrates each element and the way they combine to make the whole.

## 'Only a Game' by Ruth Starke (pp.121–40)

**Summary:** *It has been arranged for the cricket team from North Illaba Primary School (the Nips) to play against a cricket team comprising of children who reside at Braeburn's Alternative Place of Detention (the Apods), government housing for asylum seekers. The Nips' captain, Lan, is keen for his stronger team to play their best, but is advised by various adults to give the Apods the win in order to boost morale. The captain of the Apods sees this as insulting, preferring a fair game where the best team will win. The Nips defeat the Apods, and Lan learns a lesson about the importance of an honourable win.*

Starke's story celebrates multiculturalism in Australia, while alerting readers to some of the conditions in which asylum seekers live. She uses the North Illaba Primary School cricket team's visit to the Braeburn 'Alternative Place of Detention' (p.127) to showcase ideas of acceptance, discovery and community.

Through a series of comparisons early in the story, Starke encourages readers to draw connections between their lives and that of asylum seekers. This aims to bridge any perceived gaps between lives, interests, customs and values. She explores the number of cultural backgrounds within the Nips team and the ways that they have tried to integrate into Australian society through things like sport and reading. Starke also highlights the typical Australian love of sport, in this case cricket, and how it can unite individuals of any background.

Lan, a Vietnamese boy who is captain of the Nips, learns valuable lessons about integrity and good sportsmanship. He also learns the value of pride and how throwing a game out of pity for the opposition can be perceived as condescending and immoral. Starke uses the principal (Mr Drummond) and cricket coach (Clarice 'Spinner' McGinty) as foils, each with competing views on good sportsmanship. Mr Drummond implies that Lan should let the other team win, while Spinner endorses playing an honourable game.

### Key vocabulary

*Asylum seeker:* a person who is seeking protection (asylum) in another country because staying in their homeland poses a threat to their life and wellbeing.

***Q*** 'Don't lose your moral compass' (p.127). Would it have been immoral for the Nips to let the Apods win the cricket match? Why or why not?

***Q*** Write a newspaper article reporting on the cricket match between the North Illaba Primary School's cricket team and that of the asylum seekers at Braeburn.

## 'Stark's Statues' by Tohby Riddle (pp.143–52)

**Summary:** *This piece is in the form of a commentary on a series of seven albumen prints taken from 'documentary photographer' (p.143) Willard Stark's glass plate negatives. Each print depicts 'uncommon or unusual statues' (p.143) such as: a statue of a ghost cow in 'a rare moment of visibility' (p.144); statues where the whole statue or part of it appears to be in motion; a statue that seems to be levitating above its plinth; and a statue that appears to wander the world.*

Riddle's 'Stark's Statues' is one of the few inclusions in the collection not to take the form of a short story or poem. Instead, it is a prose piece with visual accompaniments, introducing and commenting on the photographic works of Willard Stark. Through the seven albumen prints,

Riddle highlights the importance of celebrating 'the uncommon and the irregular' (p.143). This applies not only to the photographs, but also to the skill and interest of Stark as photographer.

### Key vocabulary

*Albumen print:* a type of photographic print on paper coated with the whites of eggs (albumen).

*Moot:* having no practical relevance.

*Plinth:* a low square base or pedestal, which columns or statues sit on.

***Q*** How are the photographs revealing of the personality and values of the photographer?

***Q*** Research, or invent, a little-known person, story or feature within your local community. Create a brochure that provides an introduction and commentary to your chosen topic.

## 'Snow Falls on the Subway' by Yoon Zelim (p.155)

**Summary:** *A group of commuters on a subway are united by the wonder and gratitude they experience as they see the snow falling.*

Zelim's poem 'Snow Falls on the Subway', translated by Chae-Pyong Song and Anne Rashid, celebrates the connection shared by a group of strangers on a train. The subway rises 'above ground momentarily' in order 'to cross the river' (p.155). Thus, one form of nature (the river) makes way for the enjoyment of another (the snow). Zelim focuses on seven of the train passengers, portraying how each is drawn out of an implied negative state into a more positive one. Through these physical and mental transitions, he acknowledges the place that wonder has in life and how this sparks gratitude and appreciation for small things that may sometimes be taken for granted.

The passengers are united in their appreciation for the falling snow, something that is emphasised through the absence of punctuation throughout the poem. Although Zelim uses a few capital letters to indicate the start of a new idea, in not using punctuation between these, the experiences of these passengers flow from one to the next, connecting their journeys as one.

***Q*** Why do you think these passengers 'are grateful / when the subway comes above ground momentarily' (p.155)?

***Q*** Adapt this poem into a graphic short story. Consider the way that written and visual language work together to communicate an idea or emotional response from the reader.

## 'Introducing Wendy' by Oliver Phommavanh (pp.159–67)

**Summary:** *Benny is vehemently opposed to the idea of being set up on a date by his friends Dave and Bryan. He is eventually convinced to join them at a cafe so that he can meet Wendy, a friend of Bryan's girlfriend. After berating a girl (who he mistakenly assumes is Wendy) for her choice in literature, Benny is alerted to the presence of 'a gorgeous girl with a killer smile' (p.167). The new girl sits before him, and he meets the real Wendy.*

Phommavanh presents a character who wishes to remain in simpler times of childhood, seemingly averse to the complexities that growing up brings, such as romance. Benny preferred when he and his friends 'were back in primary school, talking about less complicated things like Pokémon' (p.160). Phommavanh explores ideas related to confidence and belonging, as well as the self-acceptance that needs to precede acceptance by others. Feeling inferior due to his status as 'an awkward nerd', 'shy' and 'a bookworm' (p.160), Benny lacks courage in talking to girls. He feels like 'they always talk through [him]' and that 'anything would be better than being set up' (p.160). In the end, after insulting the girl he mistook to be Wendy, Benny learns an important lesson about acceptance and the need to take time to get to know people, and to have new experiences, before passing judgement.

***Q*** Compare Bryan and Dave. What role do they each seem to play in Benny's life?

***Q*** 'Just be yourself' (p.164). Why can this be difficult, especially during adolescence?

## 'Smarty' by Doug MacLeod (pp.171–9)

**Summary:** *An unnamed narrator, who is failing academically at school, arrives at Lost and Found and takes a 'tiny book of brightest green' (p.172) that doesn't belong to him. Discovering that this stolen book will grant him 'most any wish at all' (p.173), he wishes to be the smartest child in the world. There are disastrous consequences until he learns the error of his ways and returns the book to Lost and Found, where he is granted an additional wish that returns his world to the way it was.*

While ostensibly about a young boy's quest to defy the revelations of his 'awful school report' (p.172), MacLeod's humorous poem also showcases the boy's gradual self-acceptance. After wishing to be 'the smartest kid / That ever walked the Earth' (p.174), the boy's current level of academic intelligence becomes the barometer for the highest intelligence on Earth. Horrified at the subsequent actions of his parents, teacher and peers, as well as reports on the news, the boy realises that his supposedly unimpressive intelligence is nothing compared to all the embarrassing and nonsensical behaviour he sees around him; he is comforted that at least he never behaves in these ways. Once his wish is reversed, MacLeod emphasises that contentment can be found when the boy goes 'back to being [him]' (p.179), thus celebrating self-acceptance.

The poem also conveys the significant detrimental effects that unhelpful labels, such as 'idiot' and needing to 'grow a brain' (p.173), have on a young person's sense of self and their self-esteem. The boy admits that such treatment from trusted adults in his life leaves his 'spirits extra low' (p.173). He later draws attention to the 'kind and gentle' (p.178) way he was spoken to by the rightful owner of the green book, despite having stolen it from him. This highlights the impact that goodwill has on a young person's development.

**Q** How does this story highlight the need to be careful with one's words?

**Q** Create an additional stanza for either the news report detailing unusual events, or the incorrect ramblings of the class teacher.

## 'Smiley' by Doug MacLeod (pp.180–6)

**Summary:** *An unnamed narrator admits that he never smiled, a fact that is much to the dismay and disgust of his parents. Eager to remedy this, the parents seek the help of a hypnotist. There is initial success after the hypnotist cries 'Yay Boo!', but it soon becomes apparent that the boy now can't stop smiling. After much trouble, the boy realises he can reverse his fate with the words 'Boo Yay!'.*

MacLeod's 'Smiley' is another poem that hides a serious message beneath humorous words and a rhyming structure. He delivers a bleak message about the parents who dehumanise their son by labelling him 'a freak' that they wish they could 'sell ... to a circus or a zoo' because of his 'long and scowling' face that never smiles (p.180). MacLeod draws attention to wider societal practices of rejecting those who appear different, who are misunderstood or do not align with arbitrary (subjective) norms established by society.

Similarities can be drawn to MacLeod's poem 'Smarty', in that the parents take measures to change something, akin to the boy's wish in 'Smarty', but go on to realise the perils of doing so. In this case, the parents are aghast at their child's now-permanent smile.

The broad message in 'Smiley' is one of acceptance, ultimately self-acceptance. MacLeod derides the parents for their rejection of their son, positioning readers to celebrate the boy's seeming indifference to his parents' treatment of him, and his renewed confidence in himself.

***Q*** 'As usual, my dad was wrong' (p.186). In what ways would the boy consider his father, and mother, wrong?

***Q*** Create an additional stanza or two that takes place in another location where it is inappropriate to be smiling too much.

## 'The Second-Last Baby Tooth' by Sonya Hartnett (pp.189–200)

**Summary:** *An unnamed narrator and their brother enjoy spending time with their uncles while on a family holiday. On an evening where the uncles go into town and their mother is occupied by their sick baby brother, the two siblings resolve to ransack their uncles' motel room as a form of retribution. The next morning, the narrator is horrified to learn that the police had been called to the motel overnight, investigating the suspected burglary of the uncles' room. More than anything else the narrator feels 'stupid' (p.197) but, after confessing to their mother, is able to return to enjoying the holiday with their uncles.*

Hartnett details a moment on a family holiday that lives in infamy in the narrator's memories: 'Whenever [they] think of Christmas holidays now, [they] think about this day' (p.192). This is mostly due to the havoc they create in their uncles' motel room with their brother, when they feel 'grief-stricken' (p.192) at being abandoned. However, it is also symbolic of the protagonist crossing a threshold into a liminal (transitional) space between childhood and adulthood. In realising the error of their judgement, they lament how 'small and simple' (p.198) a child's world is, and yearns to 'be a smart and proper person ... to know everything, ... to stop making mistakes' (p.198) as an adult.

In including a mother who shows no anger towards her children's antics, Hartnett presents childhood as a time to relish. As the mother says, with some sadness, 'you're only young once' (p.200), thus implying that there is only one time in one's life to do certain things with complete abandon.

### Key vocabulary

*Short-sheeted:* arranging the top sheet on a bed in a way that leaves no room for a person's feet.

*Skink:* a type of lizard.

***Q*** How does Hartnett position readers to respond to her story in a particular way? Think about the opening line, tone, setting and characterisation.

***Q*** Write a short story relating one of your favourite memories of your family spending time together.

## 'The Year King' by Michael Pryor (pp.203–20)

**Summary:** *Sixteen-year-old Bryn Scarfel is arrested upon crossing the border into Wolpen. To avoid being beheaded for trespassing straightaway, Bryn opts to be king for a year and then killed, as is the custom. In his position as king, he creates a library for the people of Wolpen and empowers them through education and knowledge. He is subsequently successful in helping the people create a democratic government, releasing him from his role as king, and from his death sentence.*

In one of the stories most overtly set in a fictional world, Pryor explores the nature of power and government, as well as innovative ways of problem-solving. In the face of death, Bryn Scarfel strategises a way to help the people of Wolpen to revolt and overthrow the political system. In this way, Pryor emphasises the power of knowledge and 'the power of the people' (p.219). In finally having the chance to educate themselves and broaden their understanding of the world around them, 'it's as if [they've] been living in the dark and a light has suddenly appeared' (p.213). Pryor thus also highlights the place of tradition, and the need to be a critically engaged and active member of society.

**Key vocabulary**

*Anarchy:* a state of disorder resulting from the absence of any governing or controlling body.

*Androcracy:* a system of government ruled or dominated by men.

*Democracy:* a system of government that is controlled by the whole population, usually through elections.

*Ermine:* a type of weasel.

*Gerontocracy:* a system of government ruled or dominated by elders.

*Gynocracy:* a system of government ruled or dominated by women.

*Ignominious:* earning public shame and embarrassment.

*Kritarchy:* a system of government ruled or dominated by judges.

*Monarchy:* a system of government ruled or dominated by a king, queen or emperor. In a constitutional monarchy, the ruler's power is limited by what is written in the constitution.

*Oligarchy:* a system of government ruled or dominated by a small group of people.

*Plutocracy:* a system of government ruled or dominated by the wealthy.

*Stratocracy:* a system of government ruled or dominated by military force.

*Theocracy:* a system of government ruled or dominated by priests, in the name of a god.

*Timocracy:* a system of government ruled or dominated by landowners.

***Q*** 'The library has helped us put words to thoughts' (p.214). How does Pryor explore the importance of reading and education?

***Q*** 'Wizardocracy' is an invented term in the text denoting a system of government ruled or dominated by wizards. Invent a new -archy or -ocracy and write its Constitution.

## 'The Legend of Lungalunga' by Samson Tavat (pp.223–4)

**Summary:** *The people of Losu village flee their home as they are terrified of Lungalunga, a pig that eats people if it's not fed its fill. An ugly old woman is left behind; she lives in a cave and only comes out at night so that she can find food. After some years, her children kill Lungalunga and then send out a message. Upon seeing this message, the villagers decide to return home where they see the old woman turn to stone and her children slowly sink into the sand.*

Tavat retells 'The Legend of Lungalunga', a traditional story of Papua New Guinea. The story relates the way that fear of the 'other' sees society reject certain individuals, resulting in their isolation and neglect. This is evident in the way that both the abandoned 'old woman who was so ugly that [the Losu villagers] were frightened of her' (p.223) and the pig are each isolated from those who ought to support and protect them, each living in a cave. The eventual 'heroes of Losu' (p.224) are the two sons who are motivated to avenge the indirect wrongs done to their mother by the pig, and what it symbolises. They take action rather than flee as the villagers did.

***Q*** What is the moral of 'The Legend of Lungalunga'?

***Q*** Create a storyboard depicting the key narrative points of this story. Consider the way that written and visual language work together in storytelling.

## 'Yinti's Kitten' by Pat Lowe and Jimmy Pike (pp.227–36)

**Summary:** *Yinti and his pet dingo, Blacknose, find two kittens belonging to a cat they had tracked and killed. Unwilling to leave the kittens to fend for themselves, Yinti brings them home, deciding to keep one for himself and give the other to his brother. Becoming impatient with his kitten's lack of strength and stamina during travels, Yinti throws it to the ground, yet is immediately remorseful. Yinti is glad that the kitten* *survives and then grows to be a strong and capable hunter, but forever with a 'hind leg that dragged behind him' (p.236).*

Lowe's story explores cultural practices and traditions that may be unfamiliar to some readers. It also focuses on ideas such as family, nature and growing up. As well as learning about the nomadic life of this Walmajarri family, and of hunting traditions, readers follow Yinti's experience of learning to tend to and care for another. Virtues such as patience, kindness and compassion are showcased as integral to prosperity within a familial group, which might include animals. Lowe also expresses the importance of storytelling and of customs being passed between generations, as evident in Yinti's mother teaching him about feeding the kittens and the timing of their travels.

### Key vocabulary

*Spinifex:* a type of grass that has prickly leaves and rough flowers.

***Q*** What are two important lessons Yinti learns about caring for his pet kitten?

***Q*** What lessons or traditions have you learned from older generations within your family? How have they informed the way you behave or the values you uphold?

## 'Chewing Gum' by an anonymous writer (pp.239–41)

**Summary:** *A schoolgirl pleads with her teacher to give her advice on how to seek her mother's forgiveness. Her mother is ashamed and mournful after learning that her daughter had convinced another girl to steal chewing gum. The girl is full of remorse and has lost her sense of self because of her actions and her mother's response.*

The dominant ideas in this poem, written by an anonymous Japanese schoolgirl, is the shame felt by the remorseful protagonist, as well as the deeply embedded respect for elders within many Asian cultures. The use of repetition throughout the poem aids in emphasising the magnitude of the protagonist's distress. They feel as though this unhappiness is impossible to overcome. For some, the extent of this pleading to the teacher, as well as the mother's mournful weeping, may appear excessive; however, the humiliation felt by both sides aligns with the value placed on honour and respect.

### Key point

The fact that this poem is by an anonymous writer may be testament to the embarrassment and shame felt by this young person as a result of disappointing her mother.

Furthermore, the protagonist feels comfortable to approach another respected elder, their teacher, to confess their act and seek advice. This indicates the trust that exists in this relationship and that, while the protagonist may indirectly disappoint another elder, there is a kindness and understanding here that is not found with other adults in their life.

***Q*** What does the protagonist's admission that they felt as though they 'were in a foreign land' (p.240) indicate about the significance of this moment in their life?

***Q*** Write a short script that details a conversation between the teacher and the protagonist's mother following the events conveyed in this poem.

## 'The Art of Hunting' by Brenton McKenna (pp.244–49)

**Summary:** *Bud violently kills a barni while in Broome, despite the protestations of his uncle. Four weeks later, in Victoria, Bud is in hospital with a mysterious illness that sees him with a high temperature and feeling as though he is being eaten up from inside. A few weeks into his illness, he receives a mysterious visitor and wakes up feeling better. He subsequently learns that the barni he killed is believed to be a transformed witchdoctor whose death curses whoever kills it. A year later, Bud has learned his lesson, and protects the same barni, as well as those who may be cursed had they killed it.*

McKenna's 'The Art of Hunting' is the only graphic short story within the collection. The written and visual language work together to convey a variety of ideas. Readers are first drawn to the unnecessary brutality in the killing of the barni, followed by the torment endured by Bud for this cruelty. Readers witness Bud's transformation from someone ignorant of appropriate hunting practices and various traditions, to someone more respectful and cognisant of customs. The graphic short story is another that explores the way that individuals who don't respect the natural world are punished.

This story also emphasises Aboriginal spirituality and the connection to land. There are important customs surrounding seeking permission to enter the land of Aboriginal communities, many of which are not observed today despite their existence. Respect for the advice and direction of Elders is also highlighted throughout this story, with Bud ignoring his uncle's calls to 'leave this one!!' (p.244) and efforts to stop him. Later, when asked whether he killed 'a big strange yellow goanna back home' (p.247), Bud is dishonest to his gaga. He therefore misses an opportunity to learn more about the customs and traditions that he has violated. The style of visual language throughout this graphic short story adds to the sinister and grim ideas and warnings that it proffers.

### Key vocabulary

*Barni:* a type of goanna.

*Gaga:* uncle.

*Witchdoctor:* an individual believed to be able to harness magical powers to heal or harm people on a physical and spiritual level.

**Q** How do the written and visual language work together in communicating this story's message? What would be lost if one element was removed?

**Q** Create additional panes for this graphic short story that explain what happened on the night Bud received a mysterious hospital visitor and awakened the next morning as though he was 'never sick' (p.248).

## 'A Dozen Bloomin' Roses' by Paul Jennings (pp.253–65)

**Summary:** *After having spent nearly all his money buying a bouquet of a dozen roses, the nervous Gerald accidentally destroys them in a train's sliding doors under the watchful observance of Samantha, the flower shop worker and intended recipient, and Scouse, a bully. To avoid being tormented by Scouse, Gerald jumps off the train and onto the train tracks, meeting his death due to an oncoming train. The day after Gerald's funeral, a dozen roses magically sprout from Samantha's palm. In tribute to Gerald, Samantha re-creates his fateful train ride with the dozen roses, in a train carriage whose only other passenger is Scouse. Scouse attempts to strangle Samantha; however, she is saved when the carriage is suddenly engulfed by roses and he is killed instead.*

Jennings' story is dark and tragic, and the only one in the collection with an obvious use of magic realism. Magic realism is a literary genre that blends magical and fantastical elements into everyday reality. These elements are not treated as unusual, but are accepted as natural parts of the story's world. The moment when 'a blood-red rose erupted from [the] flesh' of Samantha's left palm (p.262) marks an abrupt departure from the earlier realism to depict surreal and sinister events. By drawing on the magic realist genre, Jennings explores complex ideas including shame, bullying, gender and compassion.

Gerald feels bashful about buying flowers for Samantha, and then utterly embarrassed when he realises the cost. Jennings heightens the tragedy of all this by giving early hints that Gerald dies, such as with 'it was as if he was being strangled by invisible hands' (p.254). The idea of shame extends to Samantha, who is guilt-ridden over her behaviour on the ill-fated train ride. She attempts to atone for this by attending Gerald's funeral, where it was 'just [her] and Gerald's grandmother' (p.261) in attendance.

The identity of the narrator is revealed only towards the story's close, with Jennings positioning readers to make certain assumptions about the narrator, especially about their gender. The narrator introduces themselves as 'quite good in a fight' and 'strong' with 'a black belt in judo' (p.253). Given this description, and expectations surrounding gender stereotypes, the readers are likely to assume the narrator is a boy. However, at the conclusion it is revealed in a twist that the protagonist's name is Samantha, and that she was Gerald's love interest. Jennings also subverts and affirms various stereotypes through the depictions of Jenny, Gerald and Scouse.

Most dominantly, Jennings promotes the need to treat others with compassion and understanding, drawing attention to the damage that bullying can do. This extends to the role that bystanders play in such behaviour.

#### Key vocabulary

*Fairy:* a derogatory term used to attack someone's sense of masculinity and sexuality.

***Q*** What is the meaning of the dozen roses that erupt from Samantha's palm?

***Q*** Jennings uses misdirection in order to create a twist in the readers' expectations for the story. Write a story that does the same.

## 'A Guide to Better Kissing for Australian Teens' by Chris Wheat (pp.268–76)

**Summary:** *This piece takes the form of a brochure attempting to educate international students and recent arrivals on the etiquette involved in kissing according to Australian customs.*

A humorous insight to Australian kissing etiquette, Wheat's brochure may be a parody but also normalises the fears or concerns young people may have about how to kiss. The brochure includes an introduction, global comparisons, questions and answers, rules, exercises and important notes, as well as an endorsement from the government. This organisational structure mimics that of a real government brochure, while subverting expectations of such publications by exploring an amusing, mildly taboo and youth-focused topic. In doing so, Wheat presents the idea that there's no manual to follow or correct way to navigate the messiness of interpersonal relationships, as evident even in the act of kissing. This brochure may also be commenting on the nature of government publications themselves, and how rules and guidelines from authoritative sources should not be accepted without considered reflection and questioning.

***Q*** Analyse the way Wheat uses tone and its effect in communicating his message.

***Q*** Create a brochure for a government department explaining, seriously or comically, a feature of life in Australia.

## 'How I Taught My Grandmother to Read' by Sudha Murty (pp.279–84)

**Summary:** *An unnamed narrator lives with her grandparents in a village in north Karnataka, a state in India. Every week, she reads the newspaper serial 'Kashi Yatre' to her grandmother, who is unable to read. After a week where the narrator was away at a wedding, the grandmother was unable to be updated on the story and is thus inspired to ask her granddaughter to teach her how to read. Initially unable to understand why her grandmother would have such a desire, the narrator laughs at the idea. However, she changes her mind and, within a short time, her grandmother has learned how to read. With great pride, the grandmother takes the narrator to a place of worship and gives namaskara out of respect to her teacher.*

Murty's story emphasises the independence and opportunities that education can afford, specifically with the ability to read. This is something that many may take for granted, and so Murty uses a member of an older generation to highlight the disparities that exist and the progress that has been made with regard to cultural, gender and domestic norms. In contrasting the lives of the narrator and her grandmother, Murty draws attention to many differences that exist between their generations.

These include expectations around getting married, domestic duties, independence, communication and social mobility.

Murty also subverts perceptions of hierarchy associated with families, specifically the respect and dependence placed on older generations. Here, the grandmother depends on the narrator to read her favourite serial to her and, later, tearfully asks her granddaughter to teach her how to read. The narrator is ashamed that her instinct was to laugh and '[make] fun of the old lady' (p.283). Ideas such as determination, perseverance and gratitude are explored through the grandmother's ambition.

In closing her story with an apparent role reversal of the grandmother worshipping her granddaughter – an act usually reserved for 'God, elders and teachers' (p.284) – Murty conveys the deep gratitude the grandmother feels toward her teacher. This also reveals the magnitude of the achievement and what being able to read will mean in the grandmother's life.

### Key vocabulary

*Dasara:* a Hindu festival celebrating the victory of the deity Rama over the ten-headed demon king Ravana.

*Kannada:* a language spoken in south-western India.

*Karmaveera:* a weekly newspaper published in Karnataka, India, that explores family interest matters.

*Kashi Yatre:* a novel written by the popular writer Triveni about an older woman who sacrifices her pilgrimage to the city of Kashi, to pay for an orphan girl's wedding.

*Namaskara:* a form of greeting or parting in Hindu traditions that shows deep respect for the recipient. It usually involves bringing hands together in prayer, or bowing or kneeling in worship before the person, who is generally older in age than the worshipper.

*Punya:* referring to virtue and merit, or acts that achieve this.

*Saraswati Pooja:* a Hindu festival marking the beginning of spring.

***Q*** What parallels can be drawn between the grandmother and the protagonist of Triveni's *Kashi Yatre*?

***Q*** Think of a goal that you needed to show great determination and perseverance in order to attain. How did you feel when you achieved this? How has the experience, and goal, made a difference in your life?

## 'All One Race' by Oodgeroo Noonuccal (p.287)

**Summary:** *The poet presents a call for unity and recognition of the world as one family.*

Noonuccal's poem acts as a call to action, advocating unity, acceptance and an inclusive Australia. In using a variety of languages that describe the same idea, as well as listing colours and landscapes that characterise nations, Noonuccal draws attention to the shared humanity that exists beyond superficial differences between people.

***Q*** What is the effect of the questions that Noonuccal asks of her readers?

***Q*** Think about a collection of people who are united by their membership of a particular group. Consider groups such as a school, a sporting team, a club or a family. Write a short poem that celebrates the unity that exists despite the differences between individual members.

# CHARACTERS & RELATIONSHIPS

All the protagonists in the stories of *Things a Map Won't Show You* are young people. Therefore, all the bonds with parents and guardians, siblings, teachers and others are considered in terms of their significance to a young person.

The strength and nature of a relationship evolve due to age, maturity, experience and circumstance. With these factors all playing a part, a young person often begins to develop their own values, attitudes and perspectives, independent of the influential people and relationships around them. The following discussions cover the main types of relationships explored in *Things a Map Won't Show You*, with a focus on how they affect the growth of the young person at the centre of each story.

## Parents and guardians

**Key quotes**

'You should have known she'd never understand.' ('Out of the Yellow', p.6)

'... I knew I loved her immensely ...' ('How I Taught My Grandmother to Read', p.282)

Stories such as Peta Freestone's 'Milford Sound', Alison Lloyd's 'The Price of a Sword' and the anonymous Japanese schoolgirl's 'Chewing Gum' involve parents who hold a lot of influence over the lives of the young protagonists. Abigail McNevin ('Milford Sound') and Meng ('The Price of a Sword') both feel oppressed by the decision-making and expectations of their respective fathers. Yet, they both have emerging values and a sense of morality that separates them from the standards by which their fathers operate, which allows them to live and act independently. In this way, parents are presented as barriers to achieving various goals and aims, and children are represented as agentive within these relationships.

However, such controlling parental treatment isn't always responded to with autonomy and growth, as is seen with the unnamed narrator of 'Chewing Gum'. In this poem, the child embodies sorrow and alienation following their mother's mournful weeping and physical discipline.

In other stories, the parent or guardian figures act as gatekeepers for the young person's understanding of their past, culture and traditions. Tanny, of Tanveer Ahmed's 'The Exotic Rissole', may long to have a better haircut, have 'such a wonderful thing as the sodastream' (p.82) or eat rissoles; however, as a child of Bangladeshi migrants, he must navigate between two cultures. His parents keep him grounded in his cultural heritage, an important facet of his identity, while his friend Daryl introduces him to aspects of Australian culture. The same is true of the narrator's grandmother in Sudha Murty's 'How I Taught My Grandmother to Read'. Here, the narrator is made to appreciate the opportunities that have been afforded to her but were denied her grandmother due to culture, gender and time.

Parents such as the ones depicted in humorous tones in Jane Godwin's 'The True Story of Mary' and Doug MacLeod's 'Smarty' and 'Smiley' help the young protagonists to achieve a sense of self-acceptance in the face of their parents' rejection.

There are also parents who play an important role in helping to create happy memories for young people, with most providing a foundation of love and acceptance. These parents help to facilitate a young person's interests and growth, as depicted in James Roy's 'Out of the Yellow'. Sonya Hartnett's 'The Second-Last Baby Tooth' also presents a parent who is forgiving and understanding of their child, eager for them to enjoy their childhood for as long as possible.

## Siblings

### Key quotes

'... are little sisters born irritating, or do they take a special course?' ('Out of the Yellow', p.3)

'We had been through the same fires, me and Ger.' ('The Price of a Sword', p.58)

While most sibling relationships are expected to involve some disharmony, there is usually still an undercurrent of affection. This is evident in the dynamic that exists between Alex and Kellie in James Roy's 'Out of the Yellow'. Though Alex is mostly frustrated and tired of his sister's excitement at visiting the ocean, she is the first person that he wants to share his state of wonder with once there. Similarly, while Ger and Meng's plans are at odds in 'The Price of a Sword', they decide to work together to help improve their family's situation.

Sibling relationships are celebrated in Tara June Winch's 'Cloud Busting', with the opening narrative focusing on the joy of frolicking and play between the narrator and their brother. A very strong sense of unity and connection is fostered through the depiction of their cloud busting, games and fearlessness. Pat Lowe and Jimmy Pike's 'Yinti's Kitten' also presents unity between siblings. It is shown that Yinti cares about his brother in the way that he immediately presents Kana with one of the kittens that he has rescued.

## Teachers

### Key quotes

'... Spinner had taught them that much.' ('Only a Game', p.137)

'The leaders and the teachers / And the parents all were clever.' ('Smarty', p.179)

'What shall I do, teacher?' ('Chewing Gum', p.241)

Teachers are established as people who can offer counsel and support, as in Ruth Starke's 'Only a Game', Sofie Laguna's 'Learning to Fly' and the poem 'Chewing Gum'. Starke's Lan draws upon the past advice about good sportsmanship from his cricket coach Spinner when he is questioning his morals midgame with the Apods cricket team. Although mentioned only briefly in Laguna's 'Learning to Fly', it is a teacher who gives David the set of 'pencils, paints and a sketchbook' (p.99) that ultimately leads to his feelings of freedom and flying. Unable to appease their mother, the unnamed narrator of 'Chewing Gum' is desperate for their teacher's advice, a show of deep trust and reliance. In all these cases, the stories demonstrate the positive influence that teachers can have in students' growth, in offering, or being sought out for, wisdom and support.

## Outsider figures

**Key quotes**

'They were friends after all that time.' ('Cloud Busting', p.21)

'This man in front of you ... wanting to help you / land on your feet.' ('Ice-Cream Headache', p.72)

Within these stories, outsider figures can be seen as individuals who are different from the group of people with whom the protagonists are accustomed to interacting. They are shown to offer comfort or escape from the realities of the protagonist's life. This is evident in the role that Samuel plays in Alice's life in Tara June Winch's 'Cloud Busting', the strength Ikaw offers Abigail in Peta Freestone's 'Milford Sound', and the 'kindness of strangers' (p.72) shown to the unnamed traveller in Tim Sinclair's 'Ice-Cream Headache'.

Unfortunately, outsiders can also be individuals who are seen as departing from the expected norm and therefore targeted for their perceived differences. This could be due to race, gender, class, interests or myriad other reasons, usually determined by someone more dominant than the person who has the outsider status. Paul Jennings' 'A Dozen Bloomin' Roses' introduces the reader to Scouse, who 'liked nothing better than picking on anyone weak and giving them a hard time' (p.258). He targets Gerald as an outsider, calling him a 'fairy' (p.261) and bullying him to the point of Gerald's desperate escape, leading to Gerald's death.

Outsider status can also be assigned to those visiting another place, whose customs and people are unfamiliar to them. This is shown in Tim Sinclair's 'Ice-Cream Headache' where the unnamed narrator feels overwhelmed by the extent of the differences between their home and Japan. Bryn Scarfel of Michael Pryor's 'The Year King' would also be considered an outsider, travelling into the land of Wolpen and quickly needing to adapt to the dangerous demands of the wizard Cardello.

## Friends

### Key quotes

'… they still smell of friendship.' ('Cloud Busting', p.23)

'I loved everything about my best friend Daryl.' ('The Exotic Rissole', p.77)

For many of the protagonists in these stories, friendship acts as a form of escape from various realities. These realities are not necessarily negative; the friendships can serve as a point of difference that is enjoyed by the young person. This can be seen through Tanny's friendship with Daryl (called 'Lynchy') in Tanveer Ahmed's 'The Exotic Rissole'. Their connection provides Tanny with a window into what he believes to be a typical Australian family, a departure from the Bangladeshi culture of his own home.

More than anything, the friendships in the collection are shown to offer comfort, belonging and happiness. This is true of the friendships presented in Tara June Winch's 'Cloud Busting' and Peta Freestone's 'Milford Sound'. For Alice, in 'Cloud Busting', her friendship with the salesperson Samuel lets in 'some hope' (p.23), while for Samuel it is a comfort and balm. The saucepans and Dutch oven he finally delivers are full of meals he had prepared for Alice and her family, a final act of kindness and love between friends. In 'Milford Sound', Abigail's friendship with Ikaw offers an escape from the trials and tensions of living with a father of whom she feels increasingly fearful. With ideas of marriage between them, Abigail finds strength through her friendship with Ikaw.

## Community

### Key quotes

'They asked us to come and play again.' ('Only a Game', p.139)

'It is nothing compared to the power of the people.' ('The Year King', p.219)

The sense of community that can be fostered as a result of shared interests and values, or proximity at a certain time, can be a powerful source of connections between individuals. For young people, in particular, it can provide a sense of belonging as well as affirmation. The feelings of unity that can exist within a community can also give strength and support during times of strife.

Bryn Scarfel, of 'The Year King', finds himself in a bind when he enters the land of Wolpen and falls victim to the manipulations of Cardello. As someone 'who always managed to escape either through quick talking, quick thinking, or quick running' (p.203), Bryn eventually gathers the help of the people of Wolpen to change the abuses of power. In creating a library, Bryn is able to affirm the unity and shared purpose of the people, empowering a sense of community and solidarity that achieves great things.

In 'Only a Game', Ruth Starke explores the sense of belonging and camaraderie that is fostered within the sporting community. It's noted that team sports can 'be a fast track to assimilation and acceptance' (p.129), especially for individuals who are unfamiliar to a place and its people. The Nips cricket team, despite individual differences between players, are all 'battlers' who are bonded by their love of the sport and shared objective 'to win, and ... play fair' (p.123). Even though the Nips and the Apods are competing, both teams have a shared respect for the game and its codes of honour and integrity.

On a more fleeting level, Yoon Zelim's 'Snow Falls on the Subway' shows community and connection that is felt by the passengers on the subway as they 'all are grateful' to see that 'the snow is falling' (p.155).

# THEMES, IDEAS & VALUES

## The natural world

### Key quotes

'… without dragging your gaze from what you see before you … your eyes still on the ocean, big and blue.' ('Out of the Yellow', p.12)

'For the first time in seasons, Abi felt safe enough to admire her surrounds.' ('Milford Sound', p.37)

Some stories within the collection present the natural world as inspiring great admiration and reverence. Characters become acutely aware of, and humbled by, their place in relation to the magnitude and unexplained powers within nature. James Roy's 'Out of the Yellow' and Yoon Zelim's 'Snow Falls on the Subway' each portray a natural phenomenon capable of reminding characters of the importance of joy and wonder in their lives. The sight of snow moves Zelim's characters, in Korea, away from boredom, anger and insularity toward a momentary collective experience of gratitude. For Roy's Alex, the ocean is awe-inspiring, and he is unable to tear his eyes away from the wondrous expanse before him: his 'gaze [is] fixed on the ocean' (p.12). The natural world – in these cases, the ocean and snow – is presented as something that elicits wonder and appreciation; however, it also serves to remind individuals of their miniscule place in the world, that there is so much beyond, or 'out of the yellow' (p.13).

Before shifting to the perspective of their mother, Tara June Winch's 'Cloud Busting' opens with the young narrator relating the adventures they enjoyed with their brother cloud busting at the beach. A catalogue of natural wonders including land formations, animals and plants, as well as activities that helped them savour the Australian outdoors, is relayed. Thus, Winch's story explores the joy and happiness that nature brings into people's lives, and the way in which it invites play and cooperation.

Other stories warn that the natural world is something of which we should not take advantage. Characters are punished or learn harsh lessons about what happens when they show arrogance towards, a sense of superiority over, or a disregard to, nature. In rejecting natural resources or taking them for granted, characters limit their own prosperity, or even their life. The two boys of Obed Raggett's story are killed by the heavy downpour when they discard the titular 'Two Little Round Stones' for 'two better-looking ones' (p.28) that, unbeknown to the boys, don't have the same powers to form protective caves. Somewhat similarly, Bud's spirit in Brenton McKenna's 'The Art of Hunting' is 'eaten alive by something that followed him all the way from its home' (p.246) after an act of violation against nature. In an act of mercy, however, Bud is saved and finds redemption. Nature's vindictiveness (anger) is also highlighted in 'Milford Sound', with Peta Freestone personifying the Sound. It is purported that the Sound takes Kerr McNevin's life as punishment for stealing and then selling the precious greenstone that can be found 'nowhere else' (p.39). All three of these stories emphasise the importance of showing respect for the natural world and its resources that sustain humans.

## Family

### Key quotes

'… you're kind of bored with your family.' ('Out of the Yellow', p.7)

'You are children. You will obey me.' ('The Price of a Sword', p.52)

'We thought we would abandon him, / Or send him far away / But now he's started smiling / We're prepared to let him stay.' ('Smiley', p.183)

'Later I had grandchildren and always felt so much happiness in cooking and feeding all of you.' ('How I Taught My Grandmother to Read', p.281)

Families are created in many variations. While most of the stories show the protagonist to have two parents, and perhaps siblings, there are others where circumstance sees the protagonist living with a single parent, or where family circumstances are not clarified. Abigail McNevin in Peta Freestone's 'Milford Sound' lives alone with her father following the death of her mother; Lynchy in Tanveer Ahmed's 'The Exotic Rissole' lives with his mother after his parents' divorce, the mother thinking 'it was better they lived apart' (p.81); and the protagonist of Sudha Murty's 'How I Taught My Grandmother to Read' stays with her grandparents 'in a village in north Karnataka' (p.279).

**Key point**

Most of the experiences of family in the collection are conveyed from the perspective of a child or young adult. This means that some of the attitudes and values towards family can be underpinned by the misunderstanding or youthful angst that maturity and experience often dispel.

Family is cast with the responsibility of instilling important values within young people, as well as passing along cultural practices and traditions. This is most evident in stories such as 'Cloud Busting' by Tara June Winch and 'Yinti's Kitten' by Pat Lowe and Jimmy Pike. Both these stories, which focus on First Nations cultures, highlight the role older generations play in imparting values, passing down stories and celebrating cultural traditions.

Members of families are also presented as being fundamental in helping young people to develop a sense of belonging and affirming their worth. When the young narrator of Sonya Hartnett's 'The Second-Last Baby Tooth' expresses frustration at being young and naive, and says that they 'can't wait' to grow up (p.200), their mother's comforting voice proves to be a fast remedy. The child resolves to enjoy the frivolity and joy of childhood 'while [they are] still little enough to be thrown through the air' (p.200) in their games of Human Cannonball with their brother and uncles. The families depicted in stories such as James Roy's 'Out of the Yellow' and Tanveer Ahmed's 'The Exotic Rissole', by virtue of the togetherness and inclusion that they promote, also help foster a sense of belonging for the young protagonists.

Unfortunately, not all children are fortunate enough to have affirming experiences with their families. Meng and Ger, of Alison Lloyd's 'The Price of a Sword', feel increasingly alienated and distrustful of their father. Their father's decision to marry off their beloved cousin Crimson-Silk into the enemy's family compounds this. Other children, such as the protagonist of Jane Godwin's 'The True Story of Mary', must find validation and acceptance from others when faced with family who will desert her, albeit reluctantly, for not behaving in accordance with the established norms of society.

## Friendship

### Key quotes

'Letting in the sun, some hope, the rainbow had been their friendship.' ('Cloud Busting', p.23)

'It was a rare tender moment between two boys entering manhood ...' ('The Exotic Rissole', p.81)

'Mary's life felt complete ... With her soul mates ...' ('The True Story of Mary', p.92)

Alongside the importance of familial relationships, a few of the stories within the collection highlight the role that friendship plays in helping an individual develop a sense of self and belonging.

Tara June Winch's 'Cloud Busting' and Tanveer Ahmed's 'The Exotic Rissole' portray how meaningful relationships, even transitory ones, can propel individuals to feel accepted during trying times. They also may serve as an interruption to mundane (ordinary) realities. In 'Cloud Busting', Alice's unlikely friendship with Samuel is symbolic of her drive and perseverance, more than the set of five saucepans and Dutch oven that she saved for 'three years and seven months' (p.21) to buy. In an era that was characterised by institutional racism towards First Nations peoples, 'Samuel was someone who [Alice] wanted to be around, like a blue sky' and the narrator perceives that the friendship is like 'a cleansing rain' (p.23). The importance of mutual respect and joy in friendship – particularly one that transcends race or cultural background – is thus highlighted. This is also evident in Ahmed's 'The Exotic Rissole', where Tanny and Lynchy share a friendship that celebrates their differences. Lynchy revels in the culture of Bangladesh that is infused within Tanny's home, loving 'hanging out at [his] house' (p.78), while Tanny 'longed to fulfill [his] wish of tasting the mouth-watering promise of [Lynchy's] family's rissole' (p.80). For each boy, their friendship is a safe space. Lynchy loves the culture that Tanny embodies, an attitude that contrasts with the views of people who make racist assumptions about why Tanny's family would want to live somewhere like Toongabbie.

Though there is good-natured teasing, characteristic of many adolescent friendships, in 'Introducing Wendy', Phommavanh underscores this with a sense that these friends know and care for each other. While embarrassing his friend, Dave is capable of also affirming how well he knows him. He knows to set Benny up with a 'bookworm' (p.160) and knows better than to consider someone who would read a book with 'angels or vampires on the cover', knowing 'how [Benny hates] those books' (p.161). This level of acceptance is not true for all, as teasing between young people does not always come from a place of love and care. Paul Jennings' 'A Dozen Bloomin' Roses' contains a tragic death, after the merciless bullying of Gerald by Scouse. Ready to target 'anyone weak' (p.258), Scouse is unable to accept the sight of this boy holding a bouquet of red roses. Desperate to escape this 'great big hulk of a bloke' (p.258), Gerald meets his death after running into a train tunnel.

More broadly, many of the stories celebrate basic humanity, advocating for unity and acceptance, regardless of arbitrary markers that are used to divide. Poems such as 'Snow Falls on the Subway' and 'Ice-Cream Headache' celebrate those fleeting interactions that can connect strangers, while 'Integration' and 'All One Race' are more overt in this messaging.

## Coming of age

### Key quotes

'And that / was the end / of all that you'd known / until now.' ('Ice-Cream Headache', p.66)

'... from a life / that you wanted to change.' ('Ice-Cream Headache', p.67)

'And here I was, perched on the rim of a vast and incorrigible world, whatever it might turn out to be. All I had to do was wait, and then tumble headlong into it.' ('Australia Day', p.113)

'Just be yourself.' ('Introducing Wendy', p.164)

'I wanted to be a smart and proper person, I wanted to know everything, I wanted to stop making mistakes.' ('The Second-Last Baby Tooth', p.198)

Many of the stories explore experiences in which the young protagonist crosses a metaphorical threshold. This could be a landmark between childhood and adulthood, or smaller moments of discovery and transformation that guide an individual into a new way of thinking or being. There are many facets to this notion, including wonder, discovery, transformation and acceptance.

#### Wonder

James Roy's 'Out of the Yellow' depicts the wonder that Alex experiences as he sees the ocean for the first time. After initially thinking that 'it's not really such a big deal' (p.3), when standing 'on the very edge of the country' (p.13), he is mesmerised. In this case, Alex's awe in this moment is representative of a young person realising the magnitude of the world around them and their place within it. Alex is now able to see beyond his insular life and recognise the vastness of what lies not just beyond the 'black wiggly line' (p.13) of his map but, closer to home, what lies beyond his life, interests and activities on the wheat farm.

## Discovery

The transition from childhood to adult is also composed of necessary realisations. Some of these can be confronting, such as learning of harsh realities related to death, adversity and rejection, but it can also include quieter lessons concerning broader humanity.

Sometimes young people discover that their parents are not the strong and stable examples of virtue that they expected, that they possess the foibles (weaknesses) and flaws that come with being human. For Abigail McNevin in Peta Freestone's 'Milford Sound', this arises when she is confronted with questioning her father's honour and integrity. In the end, she is unable to show outward signs of grief upon the news of his death, unlike the trauma she endured after the death of her mother. She immediately considers her prospects now that he is gone. This coming of age for Abigail is shown through the rebirth that is symbolised in her standing in the still waters of the Sound, the same Sound that took both her parents. The unnamed narrator of 'Chewing Gum' undergoes a similar discovery regarding their relationship with a parent, when they learn that forgiveness and understanding cannot be expected from their mother in a time of vulnerability.

Other young people discover new truths about the world around them, which help to inform their approach to life. These discoveries might involve seeing respected figures in one's life in new (possibly fantastical) ways, such as the discovery by the protagonist of Doug MacLeod's 'Smarty'. They could also involve realising that the end of childhood is imminent, as experienced by the protagonist of Sonya Hartnett's 'The Second-Last Baby Tooth' as they yearn to enter a world that feels more stable and certain.

## Transformation

Ultimately, these experiences of discovery can be transformative for the individuals involved. For Abigail McNevin and the unnamed narrator in Tim Sinclair's 'Ice-Cream Headache', being taken out of a comfort zone leads to burgeoning confidence in their ability to adapt to change and embrace new opportunities. In Alison Lloyd's 'The Price of a Sword', Meng learns harsh truths about status and power, which changes the way he sees the world.

Many of the stories portray individuals who are navigating between different cultures and traditions, and therefore uncover the complexities of these dual identities. In 'Only a Game', Ruth Starke presents Lan, the Vietnamese captain of the Nips cricket team, who learns many new things through the experience of playing cricket against the Apods in Braeburn. In addition to learning about the lives of asylum seekers, new idiomatic phrases and the differing values of adults around him, Lan learns about morality. This transforms the way that he sees good sportsmanship, extending this to honour in life as well. In Tanveer Ahmed's 'The Exotic Rissole', Tanny has to navigate between the cultural roots of his Bangladeshi migrant family within his home and the dominant Australian culture in which he is being raised. He feels self-conscious, 'embarrassed that [his] house always smelt like curry' (p.78) and baffled by the assumptions people make about the conditions that his family left in Bangladesh. However, the response from his best friend Lynchy and the way he 'seemed to love hanging out at [Tanny's] house' (p.78), coupled with the esteem in which he holds their friendship, means that Tanny feels more accepting of these facets of his identity.

### Acceptance

Other stories within the collection highlight the importance of acceptance, not just of others but also of the self. This is an important feature of a young person's coming of age, as it brings with it a sense of self-assurance and confidence that provides a strong foundation from which to build an identity.

Poems such as Jane Godwin's 'The True Story of Mary' and Doug MacLeod's 'Smiley' and 'Smarty' show how an individual can achieve a level of self-acceptance, in spite of how they are treated by others. All the children in these poems are rejected by their parents as a result of perceived aberrations from a norm. Mary, who has an inclination to 'stand on her head' (p.87), is left to fend for herself in a desert. Here, in an environment where 'she could amble wherever she liked / There was nobody there not to let her' (p.90), she feels complete. Mary and her new friends – the mouse, the camel and the lizard – discover 'their own way to live' (p.92) and Mary feels comfortable and self-assured in this environment. Similarly, the unnamed protagonists of 'Smiley' and 'Smarty' are made to feel inferior by their parents for, respectively, having a 'long and scowling' face (p.180) and needing to, supposedly, 'grow a brain' (p.173). However, after a variety of trials, each is able to achieve a level of self-acceptance and live bemused by the very people who once criticised them.

In a very different manner, Ruth Starke's 'Only a Game' and Oliver Phommavanh's 'Introducing Wendy' highlight the ways that acceptance of other people can go far in creating a cohesive community. In Starke's story, Lan and his cricket teammates travel to an Alternative Place of Detention in Braeburn to play cricket against children detained there with their families. A series of comparisons between the lives and interests of these seemingly distinct groups are created in order to help readers, and the characters of the story, realise that there is very little that actually divides them. Fairness and morality are also emphasised throughout this story as a means of adding to the message of acceptance. Benny, the protagonist of 'Introducing Wendy', learns to be more open-minded when meeting and making new friends. This is an indirect lesson to be more accepting of his own interests and personality.

## Key point

Ultimately, a strong message of celebrating collective humanity is communicated through the poems 'Integration' by Jack Davis and 'All One Race' by Oodgeroo Noonuccal, the highest form of acceptance.

## Expectations versus reality

### Key quotes

'You've read it described that way before – breathing – but now you understand.' ('Out of the Yellow', p.12)

'You weren't expecting / to find so much difference.' ('Ice-Cream Headache', p.69)

'They would marvel at our cleverness, and also at our mischievousness.' ('The Second-Last Baby Tooth', p.196)

Connected to the idea of coming of age is the way one can sometimes be confronted by a disconnect between expectations and reality. This can occur in a positive way; however, more often than not, it has a negative impact and can result in the learning of harsh truths.

Most of the time, when reality does not align with one's expectations, it affords the individual an opportunity to learn why this disparity exists. They may learn something about their own values and attitudes, or their world view is broadened to understand forces that are beyond them. At other times, it can energise an individual to engage with unexpected circumstances.

Both James Roy's 'Out of the Yellow' and Tim Sinclair's 'Ice-Cream Headache' involve young people embarking on a trip. They have contrasting expectations: Alex thinks his first visit to the ocean is 'not really such a big deal' (p.3), while the unnamed narrator of Sinclair's poem has 'no doubts in [their] mind' that they are 'leaving behind / [their] everyday life / with its everyday problems' (p.67). Neither of their expectations align with reality. Alex is transfixed by the ocean and the prospect of all that lies beyond, while Sinclair's narrator is overcome by how 'nothing is working out / like [they] planned' (p.66). The repetition of variations on the idea of difference adds to the extent of being overwhelmed.

Meng, in Alison Lloyd's 'The Price of a Sword', has a crueller experience of expectations not matching reality. He and his brother share a quest to regain honour and status that was lost when the Qin family came to power. In approaching their father for his support, they expect that he will 'give away the ancestral bronze' (p.60) to help Ger gain entry to the military academy. The reality, however, sees them lose their beloved cousin Crimson-Silk, who is forced to marry into the Qin family. Meng feels that they have ultimately paid a higher price than was warranted, and is regretful.

On a different level, Sonya Hartnett's 'The Second-Last Baby Tooth' presents two children innocently getting into mischief while their uncles go into town for an evening. Feeling 'grief-stricken' (p.192) and abandoned, the children ransack their uncles' motel room, holding innocent expectations that their uncles 'would try to be cross, but really they'd be chuckling and shaking their heads the way adults do when something makes them mad but also makes them laugh' (p.196). Unfortunately, the two children awake the next day to learn that the police had been called for the suspected burglary of the same room. Such a stark difference between expectations and reality sparks an emotional crisis for the elder child, who feels 'stupid' (p.197) and naive.

# DIFFERENT INTERPRETATIONS

Different interpretations arise from different responses to a text. Over time, a text will evoke a wide range of responses from its readers, who may come from various social or cultural groups and live in very different places and historical periods. Responses by critics and reviewers can be published in newspapers, journals and books, both online and in print. They can also be expressed in discussions among readers in the media, classrooms, book groups and so on.

While there is no single correct reading or interpretation of a text, it is important to understand that an interpretation is more than a personal opinion – it is the justification of a point of view on the text. To present an interpretation of a text based on your point of view, you must use a logical argument and support it with relevant evidence from the text.

## Critical viewpoints

John Cohen, reviewer for *Reading Time,* applauds La Marca and Macintyre for presenting a collection of stories sure to appeal to a broad range of readers. Impressed by the diversity of voices, and the mix of new and established writers, Cohen celebrates the collection as reaching 'wonderful literary heights' (Cohen 2012). He is certain that these stories will appeal to a broad range of young readers, as many are 'emotionally charged', while others 'leave the reader with a sense of wonder and delight'. He attributes the success of this collection to Macintyre and La Marca's close knowledge and appreciation of the literature that teenagers seek, being 'finely attuned to the adolescent mind'.

Other reviewers are equally impressed by the diversity of the contributions and contributors to the collection, drawing attention to the number of inclusions by First Nations authors. Cara-Jane Shipp endorses the way the stories provide a platform for various First Nations customs and traditions to be presented, but she suggests that some of the content may be difficult to explain to young readers, particularly some of the nuances of 'The Art of Hunting'. Shipp sees the collection as a missed opportunity to include more voices of First Nations authors who are yet to establish themselves with wider audiences, referring to writers such as Jack Davis and Oodgeroo Noonuccal as having already crossed to the 'mainstream' (Shipp 2012).

## Two interpretations

**Interpretation 1: *Things a Map Won't Show You* presents the natural world as vengeful.**

Within the collection, those who express wonder and delight in the world around them are shown to be rewarded for their respect, whereas those who think themselves superior to the might of the natural world, or who appear to take it for granted, are punished.

Young people, such as Alex in James Roy's 'Out of the Yellow' and the unnamed narrator in Ursula Dubosarsky's 'Australia Day', are awakened to the wondrous possibilities of their life and their sense of place through the natural world that they see around them. Alex stands in the place 'where Australia ends and the rest of the world begins' (p.13) and is humbled by the majesty and wonder of the ocean and all that it represents. Similarly, after grappling with existential questions of life and death, the naive protagonist of 'Australia Day' looks to the night sky and sees the 'years of [their] life ... stretching off into the extraordinary distance, constantly moving forward' (p.113). Like Alex, they realise that they are 'perched on the rim of a vast and incorrigible world' (p.113). In this way, the natural world proves to be inviting, encouraging and wondrous.

However, in the majority of stories that portray the natural world as a character with its own power and will, humans who disrespect its force are subsequently punished. One of the stories that explores this idea is

Peta Freestone's 'Milford Sound'. Despite the warnings from his daughter that 'the Sound loves the fierce winters' (p.32) and the implication that it literally *'feeds* on them' (p.32), Kerr McNiven treats the Sound with disrespect, using it for his own material benefit. According to Ikaw, a Māori boy who shares stories of the gods with Abigail, Kerr has 'brought the anger of the gods down on his family: first by stealing [the greenstone] and then by selling it' (p.39). Ultimately, Kerr is killed by the Sound.

A similar tragic fate is brought to the two boys of Obed Raggett's 'The Two Little Round Stones', who take the protection of the natural world for granted. After enjoying two nights of shelter provided by the little round stones that transform into caves, the boys reject these stones in favour of 'two better-looking ones' (p.28). These new stones do not have the same power as the previous ones, and so, in the absence of any shelter from the heavy rain, the two boys are killed. In discarding natural resources, they lose the protection that these can bring.

In a different way, nature takes revenge on the cruel character Scouse in Paul Jennings' 'A Dozen Bloomin' Roses'. He scorns Gerald, labelling him 'the little fairy clutching his invisible flowers' (p.260) and later directs similar derision to Samantha, mocking her as 'another sap. Another creep who buys flowers' (p.263). However, the magic realism of Jennings' story sees the roses turn against Scouse. The roses' 'long tendrils wound around Scouse's legs and arms. And neck. Tighter and tighter they drew around the hapless man's throat' (p.264) until they killed him.

**Interpretation 2: The stories in *Things a Map Won't Show You* celebrate the role that wonder plays in life.**

Most of these stories focus on a young person's coming of age. They suggest that, though this experience can be fraught with difficulty, a sense of wonder is important. During one's formative years, wonder can aid self-discovery, make one more accepting of others and help one be more engaged with the world around them. A sense of wonder can include staying open-minded about people, events or circumstances, and avoiding judgement or prejudice that may preclude new understandings and opportunities.

James Roy's Alex in 'Out of the Yellow', Sofie Laguna's David in 'Learning to Fly' and Peta Freestone's Abigail McNevin in 'Milford Sound' are all awakened to new possibilities because of a sense of awe. Though Alex is initially reluctant to show any eagerness in relation to his family's first holiday to the coast, his fascination emerges once he faces the magnitude and expanse of the ocean, and he is transfixed. Similarly, for David, his ability to dream of freedom and expression makes him open to the possibilities that drawing and painting can bring him. Though competing against the attitudes of her father, as well as their shared grief, Abigail appreciates learning about the customs and beliefs that are embedded in the land that they now call home. It means that she is more attuned to their relationship with nature and the respect that is needed. Following her father's death, Abigail steps into the water of the Sound: 'the ripples subsided, the Sound was still' (p.47), as though the Sound is allowing her a rebirth, a new beginning. Thus, wonder is celebrated as something that opens opportunities and even protects.

The collection also includes many characters who find themselves in new and challenging circumstances. Among others, in 'Ice-Cream Headache' by Tim Sinclair, an unnamed traveller in Japan is overwhelmed as they 'weren't expecting / to find so much difference' (p.69). The Nips captain Lan, in Ruth Starke's 'Only a Game', is confronted with a moral dilemma when he realises that a win over the Apods would jeopardise the latter's opportunity to earn points and therefore additional food rations. Paul Jennings' Samantha in 'A Dozen Bloomin' Roses' is ashamed by her betrayal of Gerald when she smiled at his misfortune on the train. What unites these three experiences is that all three characters wrestle with their uncertainty but also remain open to learning. Therefore, the overwhelmed traveller, the young cricket captain and the mourning florist are all transformed by their experiences and eventually better off for it.

A sense of wonder is also aligned with acceptance. The poems 'Integration' by Jack Davis and 'All One Race' by Oodgeroo Noonuccal are testament to the role that wonder, and therefore embracing and appreciating diversity, can have in uniting groups.

# QUESTIONS & ANSWERS

This section focuses on your own analytical writing on the text, and gives you strategies for producing high-quality responses in your coursework and exam essays.

## Essay writing – an overview

An essay on a literary work is a formal and serious piece of writing that presents your point of view on the text, usually in response to a given topic. Your 'point of view' in an essay is your interpretation of the meaning of the text's language, structure, characters, situations and events, supported by detailed analysis of textual evidence.

### Analyse – don't summarise

In your essays it is important to avoid simply summarising what happens in a text.

- A **summary** is a description or paraphrase (retelling in different words) of the characters and events. For example: 'Macbeth has a horrifying vision of a dagger dripping with blood before he goes to murder King Duncan.'
- An **analysis** is an explanation of the real meaning or significance that lies 'beneath' the text's words (and images, for a film). For example: 'Macbeth's vision of a bloody dagger shows how deeply uneasy he is about the violent act he is contemplating, and conveys his sense that supernatural forces are impelling him to act.'

A limited amount of summary is sometimes necessary to let your reader know which part of the text you wish to discuss. However, always keep this to a minimum and follow it immediately with your analysis of what this part of the text is really telling us.

### Plan your essay

Carefully plan your essay so that you have a clear idea of what you are going to say. The plan ensures that your ideas flow logically, your argument remains consistent and you stay on topic. An essay plan should be a list of **brief dot points** covering no more than half a page.

- Include your central argument or main contention – a concise statement of your overall response to the topic.
- Write three or four dot points for each paragraph, indicating the main idea and evidence/examples from the text. In your essay you will need to *expand* on these points and *analyse* the evidence.

### Structure your essay

An essay is a complete, self-contained piece of writing. It has a clear beginning (the introduction), middle (several body paragraphs) and end (the last paragraph or conclusion). It must also have a central argument that runs throughout, linking each paragraph to form a coherent whole. See examples of introductions and conclusions in the 'Analysing a sample topic' and 'Sample answer' sections.

**The introduction establishes your overall response to the topic**. It includes your main contention and outlines the main evidence you will refer to in the course of the essay. Write your introduction *after* you have done a plan and *before* you write the rest of the essay.

**The body paragraphs argue your case**. They present evidence from the text and explain how this evidence supports your argument. Each body paragraph needs:

- a strong **topic sentence** (usually the first sentence) that states the main point being made in the paragraph
- **evidence** from the text, including some brief quotations
- **analysis** of the textual evidence, with **explanation** of its significance and how it supports your argument
- **links back to the topic** in one or more statements, usually towards the end of the paragraph.

Connect the body paragraphs so that your discussion flows smoothly. Use some linking words and phrases such as 'similarly' and 'on the other hand', though don't start every paragraph like this. Another strategy is to use a significant word from the last sentence of one paragraph in the first sentence of the next.

Use key terms from the topic – or synonyms for them – throughout, so the relevance of your discussion to the topic is always clear.

**The conclusion ties everything together and finishes the essay.** It includes strong statements that emphasise your central argument and provide a clear response to the topic.

Avoid simply restating the points made earlier in the essay – this will end on a very flat note and imply that you have run out of ideas and vocabulary. The conclusion should be a logical extension of what you have written, not just a repetition or summary of it. Writing an effective conclusion can be a challenge. Try using these tips:

- Start by linking back to the final sentence of the second-last paragraph, rather than leaping to your main contention straight away – this helps your writing to flow.
- Use synonyms and expressions with equivalent meanings to vary your vocabulary. This allows you to reinforce your line of argument without being repetitive.
- When planning your essay, think of one or two broad statements or observations about the text's wider meaning. These should be related to the topic and your overall argument. Keep them for the conclusion, since they will give you something 'new' to say but still follow logically from your discussion. The introduction will be focused on the topic, but the conclusion can present a wider view of the text.

## Essay topics

1. "Letting in the sun, some hope, the rainbow had been their friendship." ('Cloud Busting')
   How do the stories in this collection celebrate friendship and belonging?
2. '*Things a Map Won't Show You* presents the natural world as something to be feared.'
   Do you agree?
3. 'There are no supportive or encouraging adults in *Things a Map Won't Show You*.'
   To what extent do you agree?
4. How well does the title of *Things a Map Won't Show You: Stories from Australia and Beyond* sum up the collection as a whole?
5. "'Soon you'll be grown up.'
   'Good,' I say stoutly. 'I can't wait.'
   And my mum answered me, 'Don't say that. You're only young once.'" ('The Second-Last Baby Tooth')
   'The stories in this collection present childhood as something to be endured.'
   To what extent do you agree?
6. 'These stories show that, ultimately, human connection is more important than a connection to place.'
   Do you agree?
7. "It's as if I've been living in the dark and a light has suddenly appeared." ('The Year King')
   How did these stories enlighten you to lives and experiences different from your own?
8. 'La Marca and Macintyre's collection celebrates the diversity within and beyond Australia.'
   Discuss.
9. '*Things a Map Won't Show You* suggests that, regardless of where we live, there is more that unites us than divides us.'
   Do you agree?

10 'The stories in this collection highlight that adversity is a necessary part of growing up.'
Discuss.

## Analysing a sample topic

**"'Soon you'll be grown up.'**
**'Good,' I say stoutly. 'I can't wait.'**
**And my mum answered me, 'Don't say that. You're only young once.'"**
**('The Second-Last Baby Tooth')**
**'The stories in this collection present childhood as something to be endured.'**
**To what extent do you agree?**

When responding to a topic, your first step is to identify the key words and understand their meaning within the context of the topic. In this case, the word 'endured' will be most crucial to a relevant response.

Having defined key terms, you then need to address the instruction words presented in the topic, such as 'discuss', 'do you agree?' or 'to what extent do you agree?'. Here, you have been directed to consider 'to what extent do you agree?'. This means that at least one of your paragraphs needs to consider the truth that exists within the topic, as 'to what extent do you agree?' implies that there is some truth to the statement. Following that, there is scope to disagree.

Once you have identified and defined key terms and understood the instruction, interrogate the topic so that you can explore potential lines of argument. This also helps you to develop your main contention – that is, your stance on the topic.

For the above topic, you might ask questions such as:

- Which stories focus on the difficulties of growing up?
- How do these show young people suffering patiently?
- What are some of the circumstances that add to this suffering?
- Are there individuals in their lives that make their childhood difficult?

- Are there individuals who make their childhood easier?
- Are there stories that show childhood as enjoyable?

Based on the answers to these questions, you will start to get a sense of the extent to which you agree and/or disagree with the premise of the topic. This will then be articulated as your main contention. For example: young people may sometimes need to withstand adversity throughout their childhood; however, this often results in positive learnings and growth.

From here, you develop a line of argument. This can be seen as the three reasons that prove your contention to be true. To create a line of argument, you need to show how the arguments that you present through your signposts, and then body paragraphs, build in a logical progression. Transition words such as 'however', 'despite', 'as a result of' and 'in the same way that' can help to emphasise this progression. For example, a line of argument for the topic might progress as:

- Many children within the collection's stories suffer patiently.
- However, the support of loved ones makes it easier to deal with adversity.
- Ultimately, these children are more resilient because of these childhood experiences.

Remember to also consider the connection between the topic and the accompanying quote. How does the quote direct you to respond in a particular way?

You then put these ideas together as a cogent (convincing) introduction where you organise your ideas and inform the reader of the direction of the rest of your response. For a collection of stories like *Things a Map Won't Show You*, it is not necessary to mention specific stories or characters in your introduction. Instead, stay focused on the broad concepts that frame your line of argument and discussion.

### Sample introduction

> Susan La Marca and Pam Macintyre's collection *Things a Map Won't Show You* presents childhood as a time of self-discovery and transformation. While there are certainly moments of adversity and uncertainty that need to be endured, the stories do not present childhood as inherently insufferable. Many of the children within the stories overcome difficulties with the support of understanding family or loved ones. Overall, the stories present childhood as a time of growth and learning, with most children proving to be more resilient as a result of any trials they have to face.

### Body paragraphs

Your body paragraphs will elaborate on the ideas that were introduced in your introduction. Refer to specific moments in the stories and analyse how exactly these prove your arguments to be true.

**Paragraph one:** childhood feels like something that needs to be endured by some of the stories' protagonists.

- 'The Second-Last Baby Tooth' presents a character who, ashamed and frustrated, longs to escape and emerge on the other side of childhood 'where everything was sensible, where there were answers to all the mysteries' (p.198).
- Gerald agonises over expressing his interest in Samantha and is tormented by the bully Scouse on his train journey home in 'A Dozen Bloomin' Roses'. The ridicule he suffers at the hands of Scouse feels unendurable to him.
- The unnamed narrator in 'Chewing Gum' no longer recognises themselves and 'felt as if [they] were in a foreign land' (p.240), such is the suffering they feel at having shamed their mother.

**Paragraph two:** most children in these stories have adults or loved ones to support them through hardship.

- Lan is able to look to Spinner as a model and advisor on good sportsmanship when he grapples with morality in 'Only a Game'.
- The unnamed narrator in 'The Second-Last Baby Tooth' is reassured by their mother that they ought to cherish their childhood. She is forgiving toward an event that the protagonist finds shameful.
- Yinti is guided through adolescence and learns the value of care and patience from his mother in 'Yinti's Kitten'.

**Paragraph three:** children become more resilient as a result of childhood trials.

- 'The True Story of Mary', 'Smarty' and 'Smiley' all present children who overcome rejection from the people expected to give them unconditional love, achieving a level of self-acceptance that helps them get through hardship.
- Following his capture, Bryn Scarfel in 'The Year King' gains a sense of belonging and community thanks to learning to cooperate with and learn from others.
- Abigail McNevin feels a renewed sense of courage and hope in the face of isolation and hardship, despite the loss of both parents in 'Milford Sound'.

### Sample conclusion

> In the end, La Marca and Macintyre's collection celebrates childhood as a time of introspection, emotional development and growth. While these learnings may be a result of adversity or sufferings that need to be endured, most of the stories present this as a healthy necessity in growing up.

# SAMPLE ESSAY

**'There are no supportive or encouraging adults in *Things a Map Won't Show You.*'**

**To what extent do you agree?**

The stories collected in Susan La Marca and Pam Macintyre's *Things a Map Won't Show You* showcase the complexities of growing up. Through the myriad experiences of the young people in these stories, writers highlight the importance of having supportive and encouraging adults who can offer guidance when needed. Some of the young people within these stories endure life's struggles without an adult's care, leading them to feel alienated and confused. However, many of the stories show adults who are ready and equipped to offer counsel to young people facing adversity. These adults are able to highlight important lessons and be encouraging voices for the young people who need them.

Some of the adults portrayed within the collection prove to be unsupportive and uncaring, making children feel rejected. This takes the form of outright abandonment, which results in the young person needing to find affirmation and support elsewhere, as well as the form of dismissiveness, which makes the young person question their place. Although taking the form of humorous poems, Jane Godwin's 'The True Story of Mary' and Doug MacLeod's 'Smiley' both explore the idea of parental rejection. Neither of the protagonists in these poems conform to norms of acceptable behaviour as Mary 'stand[s] on her head' and the unnamed boy has a 'long and scowling' face, respectively. MacLeod's protagonist is made to feel inferior because of this trait, something that supportive parents would avoid. In using direct speech and a humorous rhyming structure, however, MacLeod positions readers to scorn these parents, representing them as judgemental and flippant in lines such as 'We thought we would abandon him ... But now he's started smiling / We're prepared to let him stay'. Though having parents who are equally as unsupportive, Mary actually feels liberated by her parents' rejection since, with her new friends, they 'discovered their own way to live'. In another poem, 'Chewing Gum' by an anonymous Japanese schoolgirl, the impact of a parent's lack of encouragement is profound. In physically disciplining her child and being unceasing in their mournful weeping, the mother makes their child feel abject despair. Instead of providing the advice and counsel that the child ultimately seeks from their teacher, the parent makes them feel 'as if [they] were in a foreign land'. In using this analogy, the narrator expresses the magnitude of their feeling of loss. Thus, some stories present adults who are neglectful of their expected duties, making children feel unsupported and rejected.

Despite the presence of some inattentive adults throughout the collection, many of the young people in these stories are supported by adults who guide them through life's formative experiences. In the face of crises, these young people have adults who encourage and guide their problem-solving. Pat Lowe and Jimmy Pike present this in the story 'Yinti's Kitten'. After rescuing two kittens, Yinti and his brother Kana must learn how to look beyond their own survival and protect a being weaker and more vulnerable than them. For advice, they turn to their mother. When the kittens 'cried for food', she informs the boys that they should 'give them the brains of animals', as is customary for 'babies if they lose their mother'. In this way, the mother sets an example for her sons and their pets, encouraging them to be responsible and attentive. Ruth Starke's Lan, in 'Only a Game', also finds himself in a situation where he needs an adult's guidance to navigate a challenging situation. He is horrified to learn of match fixing in the game he loves and so seeks out his cricket coach, Spinner, to explain things. Starke's use of a nonlinear time line shows the connection between Lan's receiving this guidance from Spinner, and the time when he calls upon this advice by taking pride in an honourable win months later. This also emphasises the longstanding benefit of a young person knowing a supportive adult in their formative years. Therefore, La Marca and Macintyre's collection showcases adults who can be depended on by children to provide guidance.

In helping to impart life's lessons, many of the adults in these stories encourage young people in their pursuits. The importance placed on storytelling in First Nations communities helps to emphasise certain values and traditions for future generations. In Tara June Winch's 'Cloud Busting', the protagonist mentions that they have heard the stories like the one about their grandmother, Samuel and the saucepans so many times that 'they knew most of them off by heart, over and over, every detail'. In this way, while also passing down family stories, older generations present young people with stories of hope and promise that can instil optimism in their lives. Sofie Laguna's 'Learning to Fly' presents a protagonist, David, who wants nothing more than to learn how to fly, but pursuing this dream places him in hospital. However, rather than punishing or criticising David, his mother cares for him and his teacher provides him with 'pencils, paints and a sketchbook'. This loving, gentle and subtle encouragement enables David to find a new, safer way of flying: 'as the pictures flowed from [his] brush, for the first time [he] was flying'. Both 'Cloud Busting' and 'Learning to Fly' present adults who encourage children to grow and develop independently through providing stories, counsel and resources.

When adults are dismissive or uncaring towards children, children internalise this shame and hurt, which causes further conflict in their lives. Contrastingly, when adults provide counsel, support and inspiration, the lives of children are improved and they are able to find success more quickly. Ultimately, in including a variety of stories that present a diverse range of adults, both supportive and not, La Marca and Macintyre's collection advocates for the importance of young people having a safe and accepting network around them.

# REFERENCES & READING

## Text

La Marca, S and Macintyre, P (eds.) 2012, *Things a Map Won't Show You: Stories from Australia and Beyond*, Penguin Random House Australia, Victoria.

## References

Cohen, J 2012, 'Macintyre, Pam & Susan La Marca: *Things a Map Won't Show You: Stories from Australia and Beyond*', *Reading Time*, vol. 56, no. 1, p.31.

Shipp, CJ 2012, 'Review: *Things a Map Won't Show You*', *Bringing Aboriginal Perspectives into English Education*, https://missshipp.wordpress.com/2012/10/20/review-things-a-map-wont-show-you